"*The Humble Creative* sounds like an oxymoron. But in Matthew Niermann's outstanding book by that title, we finally have a biblical perspective helpfully providing theological and practical insight on the arts and their practitioners. *The Humble Creative* may be one of the first accessible books in the last twenty years to help Christians in the arts wrestle with the vices that beset us, and the virtues we must possess to wield these powerful, but often misused, gifts. This book is a masterpiece weaving together matters of spiritual disciplines, theology of the arts, and the practices of creative and artistic Christians. Substantive theology, fresh biblical perspective, creative presentation, lots of stories, easy to read, excellent discussion guides—all this gives artists, pastors, professors, and creative practitioners a deep challenge: the challenge to face the sins we artists often tolerate, and the spiritual disciplines we so desperately must embrace in order to see *God* use us as *he* really intended—for *his* glory as we artistically bring *his* truth, virtue, and beauty to the world. *The Humble Creative* will become a foundational book for everyone recognizing the strategic intersection of the priority of godly virtue and the passion to produce God-glorifying art—whether for the church or for today's culture."

—**Byron Spradlin**
President, Artists in Christian Testimony Intl.

"*The Humble Creative* provides a welcome introduction to the great tradition of virtue ethics. . . . This text provides an innovative and engaging application of the nature of virtue to the processes of creativity. This is an essential text for the creative, for the innovator in any creative arena, for the collaborator, for the dreamer of dreams, and for those who seek to understand the wondrous gift of creativity. In addition, this text provides a practical guide to virtuous living that helps mend the destructive division of reason and imagination. The dance of creativity, shaped and informed by a deep engagement with virtuous wisdom, can re-shape our culture and re-open our lives to the truly creative One who offers us healing, forgiveness, and love."

—**Scott B. Key**
Emeritus Professor of Philosophy, California Baptist University,
Vice-President of Academic Initiatives, C. S. Lewis Study Center, Northfield, Massachussetts

"Creative culture constantly demands you to look within, follow your passions, work harder, accomplish more, and ultimately be true to yourself. But author Matthew Niermann refutes this conventional wisdom by pointing creatives to another way. This clear and approachable book, *The Humble Creative*, shows readers the importance of building virtuous habits to better form creative character. This results in a luminous look into how virtue and habit formation are what ultimately lead to a fuller, more satisfying, purpose-filled life. Packed with theological insights, enlightening exercises, and numerous relatable real-life stories, Niermann enthusiastically helps artists, designers, writers, and other creatives discover and reimagine a new hope and purpose for how their creative work can better reflect the ultimate Creator's love, beauty, and character to the world. Ultimately, *The Humble Creative* is as challenging as it is wise, motivating, and inspiring. I can't recommend it enough."

—Dirk Dallas

Professor of Graphic Design and Visual Experience, California Baptist University;
Founder, From Where I Drone;
Author of *Eyes Over the World: The Most Spectacular Drone Photography*

The Humble Creative

The Humble Creative

Moral Vice and the Pursuit of Flourishing Creativity

MATTHEW NIERMANN

WIPF & STOCK · Eugene, Oregon

THE HUMBLE CREATIVE
Moral Vice and the Pursuit of Flourishing Creativity

Wipf & Stock
An Imprint of Wipf and Stock Publishers
199 W. 8th Ave., Suite 3
Eugene, OR 97401

www.wipfandstock.com

PAPERBACK ISBN: 978-1-7252-9180-5
HARDCOVER ISBN: 978-1-7252-9179-9
EBOOK ISBN: 978-1-7252-9181-2

02/23/21

To all students of creativity, may you seek to develop your character as much as you seek to develop your craft.

To Alana and Graham, may humility ground your lives, and vice be pruned from your hearts.

When pride comes, then comes disgrace,
but with humility comes wisdom.

—Prov 11:2 NIV

Contents

Introduction

CREATIVITY IS LAUDED AS one of the most valuable attributes of our day. LinkedIn, a popular employer-employee networking website, studied its vast network of approximately seven hundred million members and fifty million companies in order to learn which skills are most in demand.[1] In 2019 and 2020 the results where the same. The most sought after employee attribute was *creativity*.

It is important to note that LinkedIn's research spanned the full range of economic sectors and applied disciplines. All too often notions of "creativity" are relegated to the fine and applied arts: the artists, musicians, or performers. Yet, as this study shows, creative ability is key for a vast array of human activity. Mathematicians are creative when they insightfully apply and develop calculations to discover the most optimal way for a company to deliver packages across a city. Scientists utilize their creativity to devise experiments to discover how a disease works in order to develop a vaccine. Entrepreneurs and business managers creatively innovate their products and sales techniques, developing entirely new economic sectors. Surgeons, when faced with a difficult medical ailment, must creatively adapt surgical techniques to fight the disease. Athletes and coaches devise creative offensive and defensive strategies, innovating the game play, with the hopes of bringing home a victory. And yes, artists and musicians also apply creativity to the production of cultural artifacts.

The observation of creativity's expansive presence across human endeavors is no surprise to the Christian viewpoint. The Christian Bible teaches that God created the cosmos and all of life within it. As part of this act, God made a special creation, man and woman, and formed them in

---

1. Petrone, "Why Creativity Is the Most Important Skill."

his own image.[2] Granted, this does not mean that people are little gods in human form. Rather, Christianity teaches that humans were specially created as distinct beings with a moral, spiritual, and intellectual essence that *mirrors* the divine nature of God. Human attributes and abilities such as love, goodness, justice, rationality, mercy, truthfulness mirror God's character.

Thus, because God is a creative God, and we are built in his image, we too are creative. Not just some people—all people. Everyone, from the mathematician to the scientist; from the athlete to the doctor; from the business executive to the artist, are creative.

So if creativity is on full display in the vast range of human activity, how should we understand the term *creativity*?

Over the last fifty years, this question has generated large numbers of philosophical, psychological, sociological, and scientific studies focused on understanding creativity.[3] The results of this research has provided a nuanced understanding of creativity and the creative process, allowing scholars and practitioners to form a general consensus on a definition of creativity. As a popular formulation of this consensus states, creativity is "the *ability* to produce work that is *novel* (i.e., original, unexpected), *high in quality*, and *appropriate* (i.e., useful, meets task constraints)."[4]

The past fifty years of research has also discovered that creativity is not just simply a tool, or skill set, used to produce a creative product. Rather, the research has shown that creativity has a deep effect on the standard of our personal and corporate lives. Studies have identified that creativity has positive effects on enthusiasm for work,[5] on workplace excitement and interest,[6] on personal stress and anxiety,[7] and on personal disposition;[8] ultimately postulating that creativity is a key attribute of a flourishing life.[9]

These research findings ultimately support the Christian understanding that creativity is a key part of a flourishing life—a life which serves as

2. Gen 1:27.

3. For a helpful summary of the extent of research, see Mayer, "Fifty Years of Creativity Research."

4. Sternberg et al., *Creativity Conundrum*, 1.

5. Rasulzada and Dackert, "Organizational Creativity," 191–98.

6. Wright and Walton, "Affect, Psychological Well-Being and Creativity," 21–32.

7. Bell and Robbins, "Effect of Art Production on Negative Mood," 71–75. See also Forgeard and Eichner, "Creativity as a Target," 137–54.

8. Bass et al., "Meta-Analysis of 25 Years of Mood-Creativity Research," 779–806.

9. See Conner et al., "Everyday Creative Activity," 181–89; Ryan and Deci, "On Happiness and Human Potentials," 141–66.

a witness to God's glory.[10] We act as a witness to God's glory when our character and actions mirror who God is; when our lives are defined by love, justice, patience, gentleness, self-control—and yes—creativity.[11]

But, it is important to note that we have a limited ability to align our character and actions with God's attributes. Christianity teaches that there is a distinction between the Creator and creation. We are created in God's image; we are *not* God. Therefore, we do not possess these attributes perfectly like God does. This theological point is easily observed in our experience of this fallen world. Our lives, as well as the lives of those around us, are testament to just how easily these attributes can become disordered. Love can turn into selfishness or enabling. Justice can turn into mercilessness or unfairness. Truthfulness can turn into lying or tactlessness. Patience can turn into fearfulness or impulsiveness. And likewise, *creativity too can become disordered.*

Yet despite these limitations, scripture calls us to become aware of the disordered attributes of our lives, cast them aside, and intentionally seek to mirror God's character.[12] But this does not happen naturally, or without effort. It requires an intentional diagnosis and confession of the moral shortcomings of our character. Unfortunately in the broader culture, and even in the culture of the American church, the average person has not been equipped with a sufficient breath of moral vocabulary to render an accurate diagnosis.

Fortunately there is a Christian tradition of moral and spiritual formation, stretching over 1,700 years, which has developed a keen understanding of our disordered moral shortcomings and their potential cures. Originating with the monastic tradition of the third century AD, this tradition of spiritual formation discovered that the first step in seeking a virtuous and righteous life, mirrored after God's attributes, was the acknowledgment of one's moral *vice*.

Now we must not be confused by the contemporary notions of vice. A vice is not simply a bad habit like drinking, smoking, or gambling. Nor is vice synonymous with "sin." In the Christian tradition, *sin* is understood as an immoral act that violates a divine standard. An independent act. Whereas a *vice* is understood as the accumulation of immoral acts and habits which have formed into a character trait. Thus, sin would be the

10. 1 John 5:11–12.

11. Gal 5:16–26; Col 3:5–14; Eph 4:17–32.

12. Gal 5:16–26; Col 3:5–14; Eph 4:17–32.

act of stealing, whereas the moral vice would be greed—a character trait. Or in another example, it would be a sin to talk poorly about someone behind their back with the hope of hurting them. This sinful act relates to the associated vice of envy. Or, for one final example, sin would be punching someone in the face, which is the manifestation and reinforcement of the associated vice of wrath, or anger. In short, vice is the accumulation of disordered habits which has led to the formation of a character disposition which no longer mirrors God.

This monastic tradition of moral formation developed a compelling image of moral vice—the image of a tree. The tree represents our lives and who we are. In a healthy tree, or a virtuous life, branches extend up and out, producing good and beautiful fruit. The tree is anchored by deep roots of humility, growing strong branches of love, prudence, fortitude, charity, justice, faith, and more. From these branches, each virtue produces good fruit. Charity produces life-giving fruits of compassion, peace, forgiveness, mercy. Justice produces affirming and righteous fruits of truth, law, correction. Prudence, or wisdom, produces strong fruit of discretion, diligence, reason, intelligence, and others. The tree is the picture of flourishing.

The vice tree, on the other hand, depicts a tree poisoned and suffering. A life infected by vice is represented by a tree that has sagging branches, with fruit drooping heavily toward the ground. No longer does good and beautiful fruit come from this tree. Instead, poisoned ugly fruit hangs downward, ready to make partaker sick. Instead of roots of humility, a vice tree seeps its poison upward from roots of pride. From these prideful roots spawns branches representing the vices: vainglory, envy, lust, gluttony, wrath, greed, sloth. Emerging from these disordered branches comes ill-looking fruit. From the branch of envy, fruits of slander, conniving, resentment, and more are produced. From the branch of wrath come fruits of yelling, blasphemy, assault, hatred, rage, and indignation. The vice tree is a picture of disorder. The roots are rotten, the tree is sickly, and the fruit poisoned.

For those of us who will dare the pursuit of aligning our character to God's, these images demonstrate a key truth. We cannot simply hope for good fruit if the roots and branches are suffering. Nor can we get rid of bad fruit by simply pulling it off the branch. Bad fruit will continue to grow despite all best efforts. If we pursue a flourishing life that mirror's God, we have to do the hard work of pruning ill branches, and replacing poisoned roots. We must dare to pull out the pruning shears and start cutting. Only then are we able to fully flourish.

Creativity can flourish or be disordered. With prideful roots, the tree spawns vice-laden branches that prevent creativity from flourishing. From pride comes vainglory, envy, sloth, wrath, lust, greed—all of which taint our creativity and creative process. If we seek to live a life that mirror's God's beautiful attribute of creativity, we must diagnose our moral vice as the first step toward a flourishing creativity.

This book seeks to do just that. This book seeks to identify and examine the effect that moral vice has on our God-given creativity, preventing it from flourishing. And by understanding how vice effects creativity, we can set about the hard work of creative character formation.

· · ·

For the last fifteen years I have been a professor of design, training people to be creative. Over these years, I have specifically trained students in the skill sets of creative process, launching them into creative careers across the United States and beyond. Having watched hundreds of students seek to develop flourishing creativity, yet flounder, patterns of struggle have emerged. Early in my career I was convinced that these patterns of struggle were merely symptoms of creative skills not yet mastered by the students. If these students could simply learn to approach the creative process in a more refined way, their creativity would succeed. Yet, despite innumerable attempts, no skill-based intervention worked. I was simply trying to remove bad fruit and ask them to tape on good fruit to a vice-laden branch. It never stuck. Bad fruit always returned. Creativity never flourished.

What follows in these chapters is an unpacking of these patterns of struggle. Each chapter explores a different vice, its diminishing effect on creativity, and suggested solutions for "pruning" as informed by the Christian tradition of character and spiritual formation. The patterns are illuminated through the students' stories of struggle. Each story told is not a single instance of one student, but rather a conglomerate of multiple student's stories—exemplifying the patterns which arise for the average student. Additionally, while the stories are student focused, the intent is to explore the universal effects of vice on creativity applicable to all stages of the creative life.

Each chapter attends to one specific vice; yet, there is a deeper influence that runs throughout. If we recall the image of the vice tree, the fruit is poisoned from the vice branches, which all draws from bad roots; roots of pride. This monastic observation that pride is the root of all other vices aligns with my observations in the classroom. Disordered creativity flows from pride. For each vice, pride is the fuel. Which is why I have become increasingly alarmed at the depth of pride which is being instilled in our students from the broader creative culture—resulting in a myriad of ingrained character vices—leading to chronic disordered creativity.

Unfortunately, over the past fifty years, one of the primary cultural messages of our day has created a creative culture with prideful foundations, and a creative culture that inherently fosters vice. This message has many slogans and technical terms, but is ever present. So as this book explores the role of vice on creativity, it must do so with an ever-present eye to this source. We all know this ethos by the slogan "Be True to Yourself."

To these ends we now turn.

1

Moral Vice and the Ethic of Authenticity

BE TRUE TO YOURSELF

TROY SAT IN DISBELIEF. The moment he had worked so hard for had arrived. Four years of endless homework assignments and exams; four years of honing his acting skills to the acclaim of the crowds; four years of building his resume to increase his chances of being accepted to college; four years of willing awkward social situations into lifelong friendships had lead up to this moment—today Troy was graduating from high school.

Troy had looked forward to this day, the day he would wear the blue graduation gown as a symbol of personal achievement and future potential. Not one to oversleep when anticipation was present, Troy awoke early that morning. He consciously diverted from his typical morning routine. Today would be different than any other Thursday—there would be no lazy breakfast in pajamas and no procrastination on things he needed to do. After all, today was the first step into the next phase of his life. Troy quickly freshened up, adorned his gown, pausing only briefly to look in the mirror to see if it was too wrinkled, and headed down to breakfast.

He was met with great fanfare at the breakfast table. His father, a respectable businessman in town, greeted him with a hug and an orange juice toast to Troy's hard work, sense of duty to his studies, great future that lay ahead. Wiping a few barely noticeable tears from her face, Troy's mother launched into her typical introduction, "I remember the day you were born . . ." Troy shot her an impatient look. Today was not a day to relish in the past, but a day to seize the future. With care he quickly hugged his mom, successfully ending the parade of childhood stories and starting the parade of waffles.

Now, sitting among his classmates on stage, Troy was regretting only eating syrup-drenched waffles for breakfast. He had an uneasy pit in his stomach. As much as he tried to convince himself it was the sugary breakfast, he knew it was not that simple.

He and his classmates were all tightly packed together on folding chairs, rendering the school's theater an unrecognizable sea of blue gowns. The theater was a longtime creative sanctuary for Troy; a place where he knew who he was; a place where he felt like himself. Yet today it was all different. In the very place he found a distinguished high school identity, he was now just one indistinguishable gown among the sea of many.

Questions swirled in his head:

"Who am I?"

"I know who I was, but who will I be in the future?"

"High school is one thing, but college is a totally different thing. Will I be able to decide what is right for my future?"

His introspection was interrupted by a round of applause inviting the keynote speaker to the stage. Troy was familiar with the patterns of graduation, and graduation speeches, having sat through his older brother's graduation. He had never really paid attention to these perfunctory speeches before. These speeches always droned on with clichés, empty advice for succeeding in life, and tortured readings of Dr. Seuss's *Oh, the Places You'll Go!*

But he felt as if he was staring down a hallway with 100 doors and no real idea of which knob to turn. Maybe he needed some advice? Troy turned his attention to the speaker.

The speaker began, "Graduates, you have simultaneously made it . . . and just started. What lies ahead is a sea of possibilities. Let me give you one piece of advice . . ."

Troy perked up, ready to receive, wanting to calm the pit in his stomach and questions swirling in his head.

The graduation speaker continued ramping up his enthusiasm and emphasis, "In a sea of possibilities, in uncharted waters, *the only map you have is yourself!* In my experience there is no real wrong answer to where you go as long as you are true to yourself. Let me say that again. A successful life is defined by *being true to yourself.*"

Troy found himself agreeing, having heard this sentiment throughout culture from movies, to music, to well-meaning teachers. Still, he had more questions than answers. "What does that actually mean? How do you do that?" he thought to himself. He returned his attention to the speaker.

The keynote speaker continued, "I trust this is not a controversial statement to you. I don't have to convince you that being true to yourself is the right thing to do. You have heard this in your music you listen to. The heroes and heroines of our movies are the characters that achieve this. But I want to help you along this path today. Let me give you three steps to accomplishing this."

Troy, being a good student, regretted not bringing a pen to take notes with. He would have to rely on the strength of his short-term memory, a skill he had honed over the years to pass his course exams.

"Students, there are three steps to achieving an *authentic life*; a life that is true to you. *Step 1*: you must become aware that there are layers and layers of expectations coming at you from all sides, demanding things from you. Families, relationships, politics, religion, and more all expect things of you—expect you to fit the mold. To be true to yourself, you must be able to see that these expectations can, and will, often tamp down who you really are. You must be able to see through them, dig beneath them, and put them to the side."

Troy was taking mental notes: Step 1: throw off societal expectations.

The speaker continued now with a more methodical pace, "*Step 2*: You must find your true self. Once you can put expectations to the side, you can then begin finding your true self. It is when you are free from these additives that you are able to find your real passions, find what makes you happy, and find your basic instincts. Inside of you is goodness and beauty which you must align your life to. Living with these base instincts is the right way to live; *the way to live an authentic life.*"

Troy repeated in his mind: Step 1: throw off societal expectations. Step 2: Find your true self by examining your basic instincts and passions.

The keynote speaker maintained his slower pace wanting to bring clarity to his message. He continued, "But don't be fooled, seeking to align your life with your basic instincts and passions is not a passive process. It is not just staring at your belly button. It is an active process. So for *step 3*: You

3

must express your passions and instincts. By expressing your true self you begin to find your voice and define yourself. By expressing your true self you begin to realize your potential. By expressing your true self, you begin to share with the world why you are unique, unlike anyone else."

Troy was becoming convinced through the speaker's confidence. Simple, three steps: *One*, throw off societal expectations. *Two*, find your true self by examining your basic instincts and passions. *Three*, express my uniqueness.

Just as Troy was rehearsing the three points, the speaker crescendoed to his conclusion, almost shouting, "Students, there is a lot of bad and wrong in this world. But from my experience not living authentically, denying your instinctual passions, or denying others their ability to do the same is of the highest wrongs. Seize tomorrow! Be leaders! Live authentically! Be true to yourself!"

Troy found himself clapping more enthusiastically than expected. Simple: live authentically, be true to myself.

The rest of graduation proved to be unnoteworthy. He enjoyed seeing his friends walk across the stage, some making fools of themselves. He felt proud when he shook the principal's hand and received his diploma. He enjoyed the onslaught of photographs and congratulatory statements after the ceremony. But most of all, he was motivated to start carrying out the three steps of authentic living this summer, and as he started his college education in the fall.

DEFINING SELF

Before he knew it, Troy looked at the calendar and noticed a month of summer had already passed. Between the long hours stocking the shelves at the local grocery store to save money for school, and spending precious time with his friends, there was little time for self-reflection. He had made some strides in seeking to express himself, and ultimately find an authentic self. After several shopping trips, he had a new wardrobe in the style he thought was most "him." But he had the nagging feeling that there was something deeper than what clothes he wore.

These nagging feelings returned a few weeks later when looking at his calendar again. Glancing down he noticed a new entry, "College Orientation Day." It was only one month away. Reading this sent joy and dread into Troy's gut. He was excited about being on the college campus, particularity since he was accepted into his college of choice. But he also knew that this day stood as a deadline to define his future. Troy was confident in his college choice, but just as unconfident in choosing a major field of study. He was acutely aware that being an "undeclared" major was not the strong charge into his authentic future he desired.

With a desire to live rightly, he set to the task of focusing on finding himself and declaring his major. The following weeks brought an onslaught of advice from those around him.

Troy approached his parents with these questions. In response, they reminded him that one day he would be responsible for raising and supporting a family. Therefore, choosing a major is partly an act of responsibility and an act of duty he must attend to. Troy was sympathetic to this idea, but remained haunted by the graduation speaker. Would it be a good and right life to simply get a job to take care of the people he loved? Wouldn't that deny his passions and lead to a disappointing life? An inauthentic, and uncreative life? Would fulfilling his duty be a fulfilling life?

The advice his youth pastor provided was to examine his life to see in what ways God had gifted him, and seek to recognize how that might align with ministry or service opportunities. Troy appreciated his pastor acknowledging his strong creative gifts. But yet it seemed the religious demands of service is just what the graduation speaker warned of—external expectations that can damper your true self. Wouldn't service taint his creative outputs?

Next, Troy approached his older brother. The conversation was short. His brother simply told him to wake up each day, and do what makes him happy in the moment. The future will take care of itself. Although this sounded in alignment with an authentic life, Troy also knew that it wasn't by chance he was accepted to the college of his choice—he had planned and worked for it. There had been plenty of days in these last four years that in no way he "felt" like studying or composing an assigned essay—but did it anyway. Could he really just rely on his current feelings? Knowing himself, he knew that his disposition toward things often shifted. Are those dispositions reliable enough which to build an authentic life? Maybe if he focused on his passions instead of daily feelings he could achieve an authentic life that was steadier than his flaky brother who partied too much.

On the eve of college orientation, Troy felt as if he had his bearings. The right thing to do is to seek an authentic life, his unique life aligned with his creative talent. And to do so, he had to strike out as an individual.

Although his parents and youth pastor spoke of duty and service, he knew that he had to find the best way *he* could serve and fulfill duty. Any outside conceptions wouldn't be authentic. An authentic life would start with acknowledging that his instincts were good and beautiful. Thus, to best serve and fulfill duty had to start with first aligning himself to his creative passions. He had to find his unique voice, and not just echo others. Then only after this alignment, the authentic expression of his life and passions would serve the world. Further, by fulfilling the duty to himself first, he would be healthier and happier, and success would naturally follow, allowing him to take care of others. To do this is the right thing to do.

Troy had a firm grasp on the ethic of authenticity.

THE CHOICE

There is a tangible air of excitement when new student orientation rolls around each year. New students and their parents eagerly explore campus, struggling to get their bearings, while the newly minted college sophomores suddenly become campus experts to the visitors. Excited new students anxiously look at their peers wondering how they will make new friends. The young students, not yet accustomed to the language of universities, ask about their teachers (i.e., professors) and whether Mr./Mrs. Smith (i.e., Dr. Smith) is a fun instructor. And ultimately, these students must complete the difficult task of choosing what classes to take.

As a college professor and administrator I serve in an advising role during orientation. While the adept admissions staff does well in getting students registered for the general education courses, there is always a handful of students who need advising on specific coursework. And in my particular case, I advise students on coursework related to the creative fields of study. The year that I met Troy was no different.

It was mid-afternoon when Troy, a tall, dark-haired young man, knocked confidently on my door. As he entered he said, "Mr. Niermann, I was hoping I could ask you a few questions about what courses to take." I welcomed him in and the conversation ensued.

The conversation followed typical patterns evolving from greetings, to small talk, to inquiring about Troy's interest and what he was thinking about majoring in. It was at this point, just as it is for many students, where Troy struggled. Sensing his angst, we moved the conversation from "big choices" to "smaller choices" at the level of individual courses. We read the description of several different courses in the creative arts, to get a sense of interest. Like many students previous to Troy, he again struggled. Choosing a course was very difficult for him.

This conversation was just like hundreds of previous advising conversations, yet it was Troy's next comments that stood out. With a frustrated and despondent gaze, Troy reflected, "How can I choose a class? Is this class me? Is that class me? I know I should be in a creative field since I have a passion for creativity. But how do I know what path to take?"

For Troy, a class was not simply an instructional opportunity to learn something new. Nor was it a checkbox leading toward a degree. For Troy, and the average contemporary student, choosing a class is a conscious expression of self-definition that must authentically align with their true selves.

I proceeded to ask Troy a few questions in attempt to explore his questions further. I asked, "Have other people, that know you well, spoken to your strengths or God-given talents? Have others sensed a call on your life as to how you can use your talents in a specific way, or to serve the world in a specific way? Have you sought wisdom from your mentors?"

Troy's response wasn't shocking, but it was unusually honest. He said, "I want to live life right. I want to live an authentic life. I need to find my own voice and not just simply respond or fulfill what other people say I should do."

Prodding his thinking along, I asked, "Is that wise?"

"I don't know, but it's the right thing to do. I want to be successful in my creativity. I need to find my own voice apart from anyone else, and be true to myself. I want to be an authentic creative," Troy returned.

The conversation carried on for another half an hour, ultimately ending with Troy tentatively picking a few classes for his schedule. Sensing that Troy and I had built rapport during our time together, as he was packing up to leave my office, I inquired, "Can I ask you two more questions?" He agreed.

"Troy, do you believe the proverb, 'Pride comes before the fall'?"

"Yes."

"Troy, isn't it *prideful* to dismiss any external influence or wisdom, believing that what is naturally inside of you is more good, more true, and more beautiful than anything else?"

As Troy left my office, he quietly said, "That is something to certainly think about."

7

THE ETHIC OF AUTHENTICITY AND CREATIVITY

Troy's embrace of an ethic of authenticity is not unique.[1] The leading "sidewalk" ethos of our day is a "be true to yourself" slogan. Just as Troy expressed in my office, the process to do this requires throwing off societal influence, finding yourself, and expressing your uniqueness. This approach to an authentic life, known as expressive individualism,[2] is seen as the *moral* way to live. The call to authenticity is an ethical call, and for the creative fields it is a particularly strong cultural ethic.

The creative culture call to a morally grounded authenticity is expressed well by Rollo May in his book *The Courage to Create*. He writes,

> If you do not express your own original ideas, if you do not listen to your own being, you will have betrayed yourself. Also you will have betrayed our community in failing to make your contribution to the whole. . . . We must always base our commitment in the center of our being, or else no commitment will be ultimately authentic.[3]

This notion of commitment to self and authenticity is perpetuated throughout the creative culture. As an example, internet commentators offer advice as how to employ these principles within creative practice. One commentator summarizes a few key ways to achieve authentic creativity,[4] which include:

1) Embracing and celebrating your inner person

2) Letting your true feelings shine through unabashed

3) Considering your gut feeling

4) Following your heart and accepting that your journey will not be the same as everyone else's.

5) Letting go of the need to please everybody

6) Making all important decisions for yourself

1. Taylor, *Ethics of Authenticity*, 13–17. Charles Taylor, a leading philosopher, identifies and argues that this philosophy is not merely a manifestation of cultural subjectivism, but is rightly understood as a moral position, or ethical system.

2. Bellah et al., *Habits of the Heart*, 32–35. The term "expressive individualism" was first identified by Robert Bellah and his sociological research team as one leading model by which Americans order their life.

3. May, *Courage to Create*, 107.

4. Williams, "10 Things Highly Authentic Creatives Do Differently," lines 45–112.

In this creative culture, authenticity is *only* derived from listening to ourselves, and authentic creativity can only emerge from the self. Any other approach would be simultaneously a moral betrayal and produce an inauthentic creative work.

This creative culture of expressive individualism finds its moral reasoning via a long line of multiple philosophical developments.[5] One of the primary philosophical streams includes notions of fifteenth-century individualism, as influenced by René Descartes, who argued that the source of knowledge is rational self-thought, and John Locke, who argued that free-will precedes social obligation. In this thinking, the individual is the primary foundation over and above external requirements or participation—which is particularly true in the American context.[6]

Expressive individualism is also influenced by sixth-century Romanticist philosophers, such as Jean-Jacques Rousseau, who argued that morality is best understood to be anchored in our sentiments and inner voice. By listening to our inner voice, we can have a sense of right and wrong over and above external moral sources such as God, or the historically collective idea of the good. Therefore, to know the right, you must know yourself.

But, as the Romanticist philosophers observed, this is more difficult than it first appears. They observed that who we are is, at many levels, a product of our relationships, our cultures, and our societal expectations. These external influences shape the self away from our base instinctual nature; they move us from an original way of being human. To discover this original way of being human we cannot look to preexisting models offered by history of culture, instead we must individually "articulate it afresh."[7]

Therefore, the process of discovering the original self *requires* creative expression and the process of making. Starting in the 1800s the idealized manifestation of the Romanticist philosophy was the artist. The artist cast aside all social conventions as a means to explore their originality and authenticity. Looking inward, the artist looked and found his impulses good, yet undefined. Therefore, as an act self-discovery, the artist stopped seeking to simply *imitate* the world around him, and turned to a process of *making*.[8]

5. For a detailed commentary on the philosophical rise of expressive individualism, see Taylor, *Sources of the Self*.

6. Bellah et al., *Habits of the Heart*, 142–63.

7. Taylor, *Ethics of Authenticity*, 61.

8. Taylor, *Ethics of Authenticity*, 62. Taylor notes that since about 1800, the artist uniquely saw the essence of human condition and became the creator of cultural values. Consequently there was a shift from defining the artist and artist works as products of

Self-discovery could not just simply imitate, but needed to "pass through a creation, the making of something new and original."[9] Thus, there is an interdependency between being authentic and being creative. Or in other words, as succinctly put by one contemporary internet commentator, "Authenticity fosters creativity, and creativity fosters authenticity."[10]

When Troy walked into my office that day during orientation, he was excited to become a full participant in the culture of creative arts and be an authentic creative. However, he was unaware that this entailed embracing important foundational ideas about who he was, the source of good and right, how he should relate to community, and what the purpose of his creativity was. Troy's rush to live authentically did not grant him the time to really reflect on the source and potential effect of these ideas. And unfortunately for Troy, these foundational ideas would prove to cause particular challenges in his creative pursuits over the next four years.

THE ETHIC OF AUTHENTICITY AND MORAL VICE

College orientation day turned out to be just the start of my relationship with Troy. As the years passed on, occasionally I would run into Troy on campus. Each time I saw him, whether simply passing in the hallway or during gallery openings, he excitedly shared with me how much he was enjoying his degree program. He would speak highly of the faculty, share humorous stories about his classmates, and, always with a smile, note that he was tired. But in each conversation, his excitement would escalate when he began to speak about how he was perhaps starting to find his authentic self. Yet, each time he also spoke of his struggles in finding a way to fully express it. Despite these hesitations, I could feel Troy's enthusiasm.

This pattern of casual enthusiastic conversation continued steadily for the first two years of the degree program. However, during his third year on campus, I sensed a marked change in Troy's conversational tone. The enthusiasm he typically exuded was dampening. One particular fall day, I found myself walking next to Troy on the campus square. After the typical update on his pursuits, I could sense there was more conversation than sidewalk left. I reminded him that if he needed help, I would be happy to see him during my office hours.

---

mimesis, or imitation to works of self-discovery via *poiesis*, or making.

9. Taylor, *Ethics of Authenticity*, 62.

10. Zhu, "Creativity and Authenticity," line 1.

By midweek the following week, I found Troy sitting across from me during office hours. Without much prompting, he quickly started to express his concern, "Dr. Niermann, I am having trouble. I feel like I am losing my creativity. I don't know why. I am really trying to be an authentic creative."

Troy and I developed a plan to unpack why this might be the case. Troy agreed to keep notes in his design journal, and return to me when he could identify specific instances where he felt that his creativity was subsiding.

Over the next year, Troy came back to my office many times—each time with a new observation. Troy would often frame his observations starting with his process of authenticity, but sit perplexed as to why it felt his creativity was still limited. Although there were too many visits to record here in detail, some of his main observations included:

- I am producing out of my instincts. So why do all my professors keep wanting me to refine and change it multiple times?

- When we are asked to share our initial ideas for a project with each other, I never want to. I don't want to be influenced by others ideas. So why do we have to do this, doesn't it limit the authenticity of my final product?

- My professor wants me to go and learn from other creative works. I go and enjoy the experience. So why do I never see what I can learn from it, and struggle to apply it to my creativity?

- My work is good, but there is a student, Jacob, who has amazing work. So if I'm to be concerned with my authenticity, why can't I stop focusing on his work, and wanting to do what he does?

- If all that matters is producing my own authentic process, why should I be concerned with how my product affects others?

- I am trying to listen to my inner instincts during the creative process, and not be concerned with expectations. So why am I afraid to show people my work?

In each meeting, we would discuss the issue at length, yet Troy always left seeming a bit unsure. But one nondescript Tuesday, as Troy was leaving my office, he asked the questions that unlocked everything.

While throwing his bag over his shoulder, Troy paused momentarily, looked back and asked, "Does all of this have something to do with *pride*?"

"Yes, Troy, I believe it does."

Expressive Individualism and Pride

Troy left my office that morning, not to return for another five months. From time to time my mind would wonder how Troy was doing, attempting to assure myself that if he must be doing better since I hadn't seen him. However, as the fifth month extended into the sixth, my curiosity got the better of me. I reached out to Troy and asked if we could met—he agreed.

The following Wednesday afternoon Troy came into my office, sat in his usual chair, and in his customary way, dropped his bag on the floor with a heavy thud.

"I'm glad you could meet today. I wanted to follow up to see how you feel your creative engagement is going. Are you doing okay?" I inquired.

Troy lamented, "I'm not sure. I'm starting to question lots of different things."

"Such as?" I asked, encouraging him along.

"Basically everything. I don't feel like I know what I'm doing. Do I really know best? I'm starting to think that my inner self is not the only and best source. Heck, from what I've seen, and what I've done, how can it be? I've wanted to be true to myself, but what if 'myself' isn't what it needs to be?"

Sensing his struggle, I sought to affirm him, "These are very important questions."

Troy continued, "And on top of it all, I cannot shake the idea of pride from my mind. I feel like I've fallen in my creativity. I'm starting to think that it is prideful to see myself as the source of right over and above anything outside of me. What if I'm not good or do not inherently know what is right?"

Troy paused, staring out my office window onto the campus square. After several long minutes of silence, he started laughing to himself. "I've spent these last years trying to throw off expectations and be myself—but isn't the requirement to 'only look to yourself' just another 'mold' or 'expectation' to live by?"

I nodded, he continued, "But this is what I've always been told. It is the right thing to do—be true to yourself? Right?"

I responded, "Troy, I really appreciate the way you seek to live your life intentionally; the way you have dedicated yourself to your creativity. But, yes, you are right. Seeking authenticity, or at least understanding authenticity defined as simply 'being true to yourself' is a particular 'mold' of life. Although it is commonly practiced, particularly in America over the last fifty years, it hasn't always been this way. Nor do all creatives hold to these same basic assumptions. Not all creatives believe that only authentically creative products come from an intentionally unrefined character."

A usually articulate Troy simply replied, "Huh."

Perceiving his response as a desire to hear more, I sought to unpack these ideas further. "Contrary to the basic assumption of the 'be true to yourself' ethos which seeks to embrace the unrefined self, there is a prominent understanding of human nature that observes the need for character refinement in order to achieve goodness and beauty. Shared across civilizations, from the ancient Greeks to Christians, is the idea that we need to strive toward a more virtuous character. And only from a virtuous character can the good and beautiful be manifested."

Pausing to see if Troy was following, he nodded. I continued, "Granted, these different groups had differing notions of what the external standard and purpose should be. The Greeks heralded the development of a virtuous character as a means to bring about *eudemonia*, or human flourishing and prosperity. Differently, Christianity teaches that though the acceptance and partnership with God, a person needs to intentionally put away their corrupt nature and seek to become Christlike in order to live a righteous life dedicated to loving God and loving their neighbor as themselves.[11] Despite their differences, both acknowledged that people needed to intentionally seek to develop a character of moral virtue according to an external standard to achieve goodness."[12]

Quickly Troy reached for a pen and a notebook from his bag on the floor. Troy's good study habits where on full display. After his pen stopped scribbling, I carried on, not wanting to seem as if I was lecturing, "So while it seems as if the right way to live is to be true to yourself, and this is what you have primarily been taught, this is not the only way. Many believe that it requires refinement of the self in order to achieve expressions of the good and beautiful."

Troy looked up from his notebook and asked, "So what does this even look like?"

"Well Troy, I think your initial question is on track. Earlier you started to reflect that it seems prideful to hold to the position that your instincts are inherently more good and more right than any external standard. I would

11. Eph 4:22–24; Col 3:1–16; Gal 5:16–26; Rom 12:1–2.
12. Mark 12:30–31.

agree with you—that is the definition of pride. So what does this other model look like, you ask?"

I continued, trying to keep pace with his pen. "I think it is quite helpful to consider the unique contribution of a long-standing Christian tradition of moral and spiritual formation practiced for over a thousand years. In this tradition, the first step toward a righteous, or virtuous, character is the recognition of *vice*. Or in other words, it is an intentional process of seeing where you have accumulated immoral habits such that it has become a character trait. Only by first identifying vice in life, or becoming aware of potential vice, can you productively work toward a virtuous and righteous character which produces fruit that is good and beautiful. And when your character is firmly and virtuously anchored in the external standard, and you are producing works of goodness and beauty, then you are living an authentic life."

"And Troy," I said, "according to this tradition, all moral vice stems from pride."

Studying Moral Vice

Over the next hour Troy's contagious enthusiasm was on full display as we explored the Christian tradition of moral and spiritual formation via the vices. Troy was experiencing a whole new set of ideas for the first time.

As I explained to Troy, it is key to understand what a vice is—noting considerable variance of the word in contemporary culture. It is important to notice that popular culture often interchanges the terms *sin* and *vice*. But according to the Christian tradition, vice is not completely synonymous with sin. Sin is understood as an immoral act that violates a divine standard. The emphasis here is on the independent action. Vice, however, is not simply an independent action but is better understood as an accumulation of misaligned or immoral habits which have formed into a character trait. Sin would be the act of stealing, whereas the associate character trait, or vice, would be greed. Sin would be the act of talking poorly about someone, whereas the associated vice would be envy. Or one final example, sin would be punching someone in the face, but the associated vice would be wrath, or anger. Vice is the accumulation of disordered habits that has created a character disposition.

In my youth, I had a friend who lived in a remote part outside the main town. While his land stretched as far as your eye could see, there were very limited city services that reached his home—including paved roads. At first, his long dirt driveway leading to his house was smooth and flat. However, over the years small ruts began to appear where his tire tracks always ran. Then during one particularly torrent rainfall, the driveway was quite muddy. My friend was able to make it to his house that day, but even deeper ruts where formed after the mud dried. Every day he would drive up and down his driveway even if it was to get mail from the mailbox, which was conveniently located within arm's reach of the drive. Then one day the post office required that his mailbox be moved three feet to the right to accommodate a new electric pole. As he drove down the driveway to retrieve his mail, he followed his same pattern, naturally falling into the established tire ruts. However, when he got to the mailbox, he was unable to reach the mail from his car. He decided to move the car closer, attempting to turn the wheel. But no matter what he did, he was unable to get his tires out of the rut. All that he could do was go backward and forward in the established pattern. His years of habitual actions, accentuated by actions taken in a dramatic situation, had rendered it nearly impossible to do differently.

Vice works in a similar way. The habits established and practiced ultimately produce further actions in the same rut, digging it deeper and deeper. Then ultimately what started as one small immoral habit, or a way of acting brought on by a dramatic event, becomes who you are. Vice begets vice. Therefore, to begin the process of moral formation, intentional effort is required. As my friend's driveway demonstrated, when vice goes unchecked, it can become so deeply ingrained in you that it becomes your instinct, your character, and your natural actions to any number of situations.

Therefore, it is key to note that there is a fundamental interconnection between what you do, who you become, your actions, and the products you produce. To borrow an image from this tradition of moral and spiritual formation, if the tree is poisoned, then the fruit will be bad. This image of a tree with fruit is a common and useful image used in this tradition. The tree is often depicted with branches representing the different vices, and from these vices poisoned fruit, or sin, emerges and hangs downward. While there are variances between different depictions of vice trees, common poisoned branches include: envy, sloth, greed, lust, wrath, and vainglory.

As Troy and I were looking at a depiction of a vice tree, Troy interrupted the flow of conversation and remarked, "What is that on the roots of the tree? Is that the word for pride?"

I confirmed his observation.

With astute observation, he began to think out loud. "Wait, pride is the root of all other vices? And pride is the undeserved elevation of myself over others—like what I was doing when I was trying to be true to only look to myself for the good and the right. That means that in my attempt to be an authentic creative, and be true to myself, I planted seeds of pride—which may have grown into other vices."

Impressed with his introspection, I softly said, "Perhaps."

He continued, "And if I have a tree of vices, my fruit may be poisoned as well. Is this why I have struggled so much with my creative endeavors? Has my dedication to be an authentic creative by elevating myself actually hampered my creativity?"

"I think you are onto something," I replied.

"To think all these years . . . I thought for sure that my desire to express my unique self would flourish creativity. How could it not? I was requiring myself to be unique, authentic. But in the process, I was simply cultivating pride, and vice in my life. And these vices produced a disordered character which in turn created bad fruit."

Troy had a mix of relief and terror simultaneously on his face. Looking up from his lap, he looked straight at me and said, "I need to get out of these ruts. Can we meet again?"

After some discussion, we agreed to meet regularly to go back over his sketchbook observations we discussed the past year. Week by week over the next year we examined his observations of stilted creativity. And week by week we easily found vice after vice: sloth, greed, wrath, lust, envy, vainglory, and of course pride.

• • •

Troy is no different from the majority of my students seeking to pursue an ethic of authenticity in the creative fields. Year after year, students from all backgrounds seek to be true to themselves, unaware of the foundational ideas they were adopting; unaware of the seeds of pride they were planting. And just like Troy these students struggled in their creative pursuits as vice grew more prominent in their lives.

Moral vices strangle good creative processes, which ultimately produces bad fruit. Yet, with humble and intentional moral formation through the examination of vice in one's life, we can jump the established rut and begin pursuing a virtuous moral life of flourishing creativity. So to that end we turn.

In the chapters to come, we will examine this poisonous relationship between moral vice derived from dedication to expressive individualism and the creative process. In each chapter, we will learn through the story of an individual who exemplified a particular vice, observing its effect on the creative process. The hope is that each of you, like Troy, will come to discover how the roots of pride have created moral vice in your life. And like Troy, I hope that each of you will be willing to seek intentional change and start producing good and beautiful creative fruit.

2

Vainglory

THE FIRST DAY OF a new class is always an exciting occasion—particularly for a class on creativity. Most students have never considered that "creativity" can be taught; assuming that it is just an innate ability possessed by a few people. Thus, students come to the class with very few preconceived notions or expectations. As a professor, I find this comforting and strategic. For a class that intends to teach students the skills and processes needed to produce novel, high-quality, and appropriately useful works—preconceived notions tend to just get in the way.

Yet, despite the course's uniqueness, the first day pre-class routine is no different. Students nervously wander into class excessively early, having left their dorm with plenty of time to navigate to the classroom, allowing for a wrong turn. After cautiously peering into the classroom, and slowly making their way to an empty seat, they sit in silence. Quietly waiting.

And as typical, there is always one student whose self-confidence either blinds them from being aware of this routine, or allows them to consciously revolt from the silence. In either case, this student becomes the catalyst. They sit; they ignore the silence; they boldly speak to their quiet neighbor. And slowly they become the permission slip needed for other students to cautiously begin chatting.

In a particularity notable semester a few years back, this pattern reliably played itself out—but with one key difference. The first day of this class, not one seemingly self-confident student broke the silence, but two: Emma and Eric.

Now at first glance Emma and Eric were nothing alike. Eric was a tall and lanky young man. He wore a smile that filled the majority of his face. Although kind in his words, his eyes were always a bit mischievous. His hair was clean but disheveled, and his clothes—nearly always a T-shirt—were wrinkled. Eric typically came to class with a pen in his pocket, and a handful of papers in disarray. Eric was the definition of casual, carefree happiness.

Emma, on the other hand, exuded professionalism. By all first appearances she was the definition of average: average height, average build, and average appearance. But it was the way she carried herself. She walked with purpose, always came prepared, dressed sharply, and was full of intention. Unlike Eric's disheveled stack of papers, Emma carried a professional-looking bag, appropriate for her age—but distinguished. Inside, her bag was acutely organized; well prepared for any occasion.

On that first day of class, Eric came in first. Without even a glance at the room, he casually sauntered to the back row, selecting a chair between two other students. Emma followed two minutes later. Opposite of Eric, she took a beeline for the front row of the class, also finding a seat between two other students. And, as typical, with these catalysts, it was only one minute later that their conversations were audible to the entire room.

As a professor, I am always glad when the awkward silence is broken by the catalyst. Once students begin talking, their eyes shift away from me—expectantly waiting—and move to their neighbor. This allows me some time to complete final preparations for the opening class session. But on this particular day, I had finished my preparations early, allowing my attention to float to the emerging conversations.

Naturally the two loudest conversations were emerging from the front and back rows, centered on Emma and Eric. Eric's smile flashed largely back and forth, as he animated his story with exaggerated gestures. The initial giggles morphed into loud roars of laughter—spurring Eric on. Soon he nearly had two rows of students focused on him, laughing, clapping, and thankfully breaking the first day tensions. In the midst of his story, Eric caught my eye. I smiled at him, hoping to communicate that I was glad he was here.

As I shifted my focus back to my papers, Emma's conversation came into earshot. She was recalling her summer internship in New York, re-counting to the listening ears just how selective the opportunity was, and how many industry professionals she was able to meet. Her fellow students responded with short responses, "Wow," and, "That's amazing." Emma didn't allow for much more to be said by others. She quickly noted that the internship provided her with several great portfolio pieces. But, as she worried, she only had five showcase pieces, not nearly enough for a professional portfolio. Sensing the growing worries from her classmates who had not even considered making a portfolio, I moved to start the class.

From all first impressions, Emma and Eric anchored opposite ends of the spectrum. They presented themselves differently; they spoke with very different tones; they were the back row and the front row. But as Emma and Eric moved into their creative processes it became apparent that they shared one key character trait. Both Eric and Emma struggled with disordered creativity due to the *vice of vainglory*.

THE VICE OF VAINGLORY

Vainglory, by all contemporary accounts, is not a common word. Thus, for clarity sake, it is worth taking a few lines to layout a solid description prior to moving forward.

Vainglory is a vice, or character trait, for which a person has an *"excessive and disordered desire for recognition and approval from others."*[1]

Like all vices, it is important to note that vainglory is the distortion of a natural appetite that exists in all humanity: a healthy desire to please other human beings and the desire to be acknowledged.[2] Yet in the vice of vainglory, this once healthy branch gets twisted and warped in two directions.

First, a person's healthy desire to be rightly admired for worthy things transforms into a *desire to be admired for non-worthy, or vain, empty, things.*[3] Fruit from these branches are not truly glorious. It would be as if we replaced a bright red, juicy apple with a poorly made piece of plastic fruit. Yet, even though we know that the plastic fruit is an imitation and empty of value, we go to great lengths to ensure that we receive praise for the fake apple. We do this in a few ways.

In order to receive praise for our fake apple, we can take our fake fruit and show it off to other people who love fake fruit, or don't care to know the difference. Or in other words, we pander to the crowd: whatever is popular, we do—no matter how shallow. We go to great lengths to showcase our

1. DeYoung, *Glittering Vices*, 60.
2. Aquinas, *On Evil*, IX.1.ad 3 and IX.2.ad 9.
3. DeYoung, *Glittering Vices*, 60–61.

fake apple in order to seek the applause. We seek approval from people for things that do not matter—vain, empty things. We seek falsely given glory.

If we don't take our fake fruit to the fake fruit lovers, the other route we can try is to pass off our fake fruit as real. But knowing that it is fake, we must make it out to be more than it is. To do so, we exaggerate: "Look how red this is, redder than any apple you have seen." We aggrandize: "This is the most important, or special apple there is." Or we provide overstated testimony: "My apple has changed people's lives, without it they wouldn't be the same." The distorted need for approval and acknowledgment attempts to override reality, and in turn we lie to cajole applause from others.

Second, a person's healthy desire to be rightly admired for worthy things transforms into *a need to be admired in the wrong way*.[4] Whereas in the first case, a person seeks admiration for the wrong things, in this twisting of the branch, we seek more admiration than is due. Yes, we may have an actual red, juicy, delicious apple—which is worthy of admiration. However, we need, and expect, thunderous applause despite it being worthy of a polite golf clap.

To receive this extra praise, we claim more credit than is due, effectively stealing glory.[5] To carry through with the metaphor, by claiming all the credit for the apple, we steal glory from tree farmers who raised the tree from a seedling before you transferred it to your field; we steal glory from the farmhand who worked diligently to keep the soil fertile for the tree; and we steal glory from God, who provided the soil and the rain necessary to make the tree grow.

Or to move it out of the metaphor, let's suppose you are a talented writer, and you win an award for your recent book. In excessively accepting (and encouraging) praise for this award, you are stealing glory due to others. Yes, you wrote the book. But you were mentored by teachers, your words were refined by a sharp-eyed editor, you were provided the time to develop your book through the provision of your family, and most of all, you were gifted with these talents by God. Yes, you deserve praise for your efforts. Acknowledgment is good. But if you seek, or claim, more credit than you are due, you are chasing after false glory.

No matter if one seeks admiration for unworthy things, or seeks wrong levels of admiration, vainglory desires attention and approval. The vice of vainglory grows to a point where a natural love for acknowledgment

---

4. DeYoung, *Glittering Vices*, 60–61.
5. Ezek 28:2; Jer 9:23–24; 1 Cor 4:7.

warps life to become about others taking notice.[6] A person struggling with the vice of vainglory will exaggerate, or even make up something about themselves—a.k.a. lie—to impress. A vain person will be motivated to do good things, not for the sake of good, but for the hope that someone will give them praise for it. A vain person will then be disappointed when no one does praise them for it. A vain person concerns themselves more with what other people think than with who they are. A vain person needs applause.

VAINGLORY AND EXPRESSIVE INDIVIDUALISM

By all accounts Emma and Eric were both very comfortable in their own skin. They were self-confident, sure of what they desired, and active in their pursuits of it. As I got to know Emma and Eric better throughout the class, the more this became apparent.

By first impressions, Eric could easily be cast as someone who didn't put too much thoughts into life—he was the back-row dweller looking for a good time. And while this description has some truth, I came to learn that intentionality was his middle name.

During the creativity course, there is a section that discusses barriers and the roles they play in the creative process. As a warm-up, I ask the students to stand in a line while I read a set of privileges or limitations people could face in life. If the student had experienced the statement, they would either take a step forward or a step back, respectively. Following, students are invited to reflect on the exercise and share their own perception and story of barriers they have faced in their creative pursuits. Eric spoke up first—to no surprise.

At the invitation, Eric waived his long lanky arms in the air wildly saying, "Choose me. Choose me—the wacky waving inflatable arm guy outside the car dealership." Persuaded by the class's laughter, I obliged.

Eric started, "Hi, I'm Eric . . . and I'm addicted to creativity." More laughter.

He continued, "You guys know me this way, creative, fun, always looking to the wacky ideas. And this is the real me. But let me tell you it hasn't always been that way."

His tone took on a rare seriousness, "Both my parents are doctors—surgeons to be exact. I was raised in a home where there was an expectation

6. For an instructive list of symptoms of vainglory, see DeYoung, *Glittering Vices*, 60–64.

I would follow in their footsteps. They wanted me to be a surgeon. So my childhood was books, textbooks, and study . . . followed by more studying. And for fun, my parents would bring me a specimen to dissect, explore, and try to sew back up."

A smile returned as he recalled, "Fortunately they were both doctors, because each time I cut a specimen open, I fainted. Code blue . . . We need a crash cart . . ."

More laughter, "This has been the biggest barrier in my creativity. I am not a surgeon—despite what my parents want. I am a creative. It was only last year that I made the call. I had to be true to who I was. I couldn't live a life just because it was the family tradition. So, for three years I joined the film club at my high school, and started making films. I would secretly order textbooks from online, and really started working on my craft. Finally, despite my family trade, and the desire of my parents, I applied to this college, to study in the creative arts. I don't care what my family thinks, I am doing the right thing following my passion."

Pausing for dramatic effect, he ended, "Hi, I am Eric, and I am a filmmaker."

"Thank you for sharing, Eric. We appreciate that you are here," I said.

Over the next hour, students followed Eric's lead in reflecting on boundaries related to creativity. As the hour progressed, I was sure that Emma would chime in. Now and then I would pass a glance her way, expecting to call on her. My eyes were met with avoidance, as she quickly looked down at the table in front of her. As the clock reached the top of the hour, class ended.

I packed my bag and headed to my office, wondering why the normally talkative Emma felt so timid during class. I was shaken from these thoughts as I reached the main campus square, lined with the vast old trees and breathtaking flowers in full bloom. The sheer beauty of campus compelled a person's full attention and appreciation. I had nearly walked halfway across the square before I realized someone was walking right next to me. I looked over.

"Dr. Niermann? Sorry, I didn't want to bother you. You looked like you were deep in thought." Emma said.

She continued, "I was wondering if I could talk with you for a second."

"Sure Emma, what can I do for you?" I replied.

"I don't know . . . It seemed like you wanted me to talk in class today, but . . . I don't know, I suppose I was a bit hesitant. I feel like my story is different. I don't have surgeon parents, or even parents with college degrees. My family immigrated to this country when I was small. Growing up, we were happy—unaware. My parents were laborers. They worked hard and provided for us. But we were poor," Emma reflected.

We paused to sit on a bench under the shade of an old tree. She carried on, "And because we had no money, family was everything. And I don't just mean my parents and my brothers. Family was huge—hordes of aunts, uncles, cousins, grandparents. So many people, all living in the same spot."

"That sounds like it could have been a lot of fun growing up," I encouraged.

"It was, I loved it. But I don't want to be a laborer, or work at a factory. I wanted to go to college, to be an interior designer. I want to make beautiful spaces for people to live and work in." She hesitated before continuing, "So I did the unthinkable, I got accepted to college and left."

Picking up pace, she clarified, "I know this doesn't sound like much. This is normal for people whose parents did the same thing. But to leave family! You don't leave the family. It is your security, your role, your life."

Slowing, she reflectively said, "But I had to. I had to follow my heart. I had to chase my dreams. The family was mad. They don't even really talk to me very much anymore. But I don't need their approval, I am living my dream. It's the right thing to do."

"Emma, I'm glad you shared this with me." I smiled.

"Anyway, thanks for your time, I look forward each week to the class." And with that, Emma got up and left.

As I finished the walk to my office, I reflected just how similar Eric and Emma's stories were. Both of these students faced a set of expectations—a mold to live by. Yet, despite these expectations, they decided to reject the mold, and follow their passions. And in doing so, they had taken an assertive stance that because they were being true to themselves, they did not need approval from anyone. Their authentic self was enough affirmation. As Emma's and Eric's story will prove out, the reliance on the authentic self as the sole source of affirmation is a false front.

It is important to note at this point that the choices of these two individuals to pursue their creative paths is not under critique. Rather, it is important to observe that there is an ironic contradiction that occurs with expressive individualism. And from this contradiction, the potential for the development of vainglory in a person's life is strong.

Expressive individualism purports that an authentic life comes from a focus on the individual's raw passions, and the true expression of those passions to the world—unapologetically. And by accomplishing a full embrace of yourself, despite any and all expectations, you are living the right and authentic life; you are complete.

Yet, as many have observed and experienced, life does not fully work this way. As humans, we need affirmation; our identities require recognition.[7] Individuals are not isolated atoms floating in space. Rather, we develop ourselves within a context. Identities are "formed in dialogue with others . . . with their recognition of us."[8] So the demands of expressive individualism to anchor identity solely in the self, causes people to redefine their need for recognition in two disordered ways; at two opposite ends of the spectrum.

At one end, when we sense this need for others to recognize us, it is rejected. In this approach, life is disciplined to the idea of individual self-reliance. In doing so, we transform any relationship into being "purely instrumental in their significance."[9] Or in other words, relationships become tools for self-development and fulfillment. Therefore, the notion of predetermined lifelong relationships is nonsense.[10] Once a relationship begins to infringe on who you are, or stops aiding the development of yourself, it is right to end the relationship. The highest priority is maintaining the authentic self. The need for acknowledgment is fulfilled by yourself, but at the expense of those around you.

Or second, and more commonly, we try to tell ourselves that we do not need approval from others. However, we are never able to fully shape our lives to this idea. The need for recognition is self-consciously denied. Yet, unconsciously, it is like someone puts growth hormone on our need for recognition. The craving for affirmation of our unique self-expression becomes unbalanced. We seek affirmation for things that are unworthy or insignificant, requiring applause simply because we have exactly 3,732 hairs on our head.[11] Or we seek too much affirmation for our appropriate, and unique, significance. Small habitual attempts to fulfill this craving accumulate—resulting in a character shaped by the vice of vainglory.

7. Taylor, *Ethics of Authenticity*, 45.

8. Taylor, *Ethics of Authenticity*, 46.

9. Taylor, *Ethics of Authenticity*, 43.

10. Taylor, *Ethics of Authenticity*, 43–44.

11. Taylor, *Ethics of Authenticity*, 36.

Like most people that attempt this path, Emma and Eric could not fully shape their life to a pure expressive individualism ideology. Their longing for acknowledgment grew into the vice of vainglory. By seeking to be true to themselves, they developed a disordered need for affirmation—a need that presented real challenges to their creativity.

VAINGLORY AND CREATIVITY

It should be noted that the ironic need for affirmation that expressive individualism produces can certainly lead to vainglory. However, by no means is it the only path to vainglory. Even for individuals who do not abide by the ethic of authenticity, the natural love for being recognized by others can easily become distorted. And in either case, once the vice of vainglory is developed, disordered creativity is quick to follow. Unfortunately, Emma and Eric discovered this the hard way.

As one can imagine, a course designed to teach creativity is not just a lecture course. Each week students are asked to apply their learning, and develop their skills, through projects. As the projects progress, students are exposed to varying levels of inputs, constraints, aims, and mediums with the intent of teaching different aspects of the creative process. Yet despite these differences in the project parameters, I noticed midway through the semester, Emma and Eric were carrying out the same process each time.

Emma would start her process, no matter the project, by spending hours leafing through high-end print and online design journals—collecting images like a squirrel before winter. While I am not certain, I can imagine that she might have taped these images on her dorm room wall, making a cocoon of high-end projects for herself.

After the collection phase, she would then incessantly nibble on an idea. Now, I never saw these ideas. Early in the process, when I would ask to see and critique her work, she would justify not letting me see on account of incompleteness. Knowing Emma, this was not the case. A simple survey of the class would show that she had completed twice the developmental work as others.

Next would come peer-critique day. During this day, students are asked to show their ideas to a group of students, providing feedback for each other. Emma would participate on these days, she was not unique in this. But her uniqueness would come after. Without fail, Emma would approach me after class asking if she could show me her project to get feedback.

After a few times, these sessions became predictable. She would come into my office, and after exchanging greetings I would ask, "Did the peer critiques today help? Were there any ideas that were unlocked for you?"

She always responded, "Kind of, but I want to know what you think. Your opinion is important to me."

To her credit, the majority of her projects showed promise at the beginning—and I would affirm her in this.

But any affirmation would be followed with, "So you really like it? Is it really good enough? Is it to a professional level? Could it be in a design journal? Do you like it?"

I would do my best to affirm her again, but also encourage her that she needed to continue her creative process and push the project further—being open to trying new ways to develop the project. She would retort, "Yes, but you said it was in a good spot . . ."

"Keep going, Emma, keep going. Try to see it differently and see what comes of it." And with that, the meeting would end.

Then, as the weeks passed on, and final presentation day would arrive. Consistently, Emma would present nearly the same project I saw in my office weeks previous. And the pattern would repeat with the next project.

Yes, Emma's projects were good—but undeveloped. She never took risks. She never tried new approaches. She cared very little for her peers' acknowledgment, but craved acknowledgment by the professors. Once she received initial recognition for the work, she was afraid to change it for fear of losing that recognition. Attempting to develop the project further opened the door for the project to no longer be considered good. And for Emma, holding onto the good, and fearing the bad, prevented her from taking the project to great.

Eric, on the other hand, never came to my office nor sought extra critiques from me. He relished in peer critiques. As a matter of fact, for Eric, every day was peer critique day. Before class, after class, and to my chagrin, even during class. At every stage of development, Eric would quickly delineate the idea and before developing it further, would look to his left and ask their thoughts; look to the right and ask their thoughts.

Eric had good creative instincts, and his projects showed promise. But when final presentation day came, the work never met the mark. The work often appeared to have multiple ideas running together, never fully resolved. Or, the work seemed to simply stay at the surface, never finding the next level of depth or significance. Consequently, I would assign a final grade aligned with this level of development.

The posting of a grade for the largest project of the semester triggered the only visit Eric paid to my office. He knocked, and entered.

"Professor Niermann, can I ask you about my grade?" he asked.

I happily responded, "Certainly, Eric."

"I just wondered why I'm getting these lower grades. I thought this last project went well. Diego said he loved the way it was framed. Kaylan commented on the care of delineation. Alex and Wesley laughed out loud and that one part, and at my presentation. And, not to brag, but I got the loudest applause of everybody. Why didn't I receive a high grade?"

I responded with a question. "Eric, you want to be a filmmaker. What was your friends' favorite film in high school?"

He responded with a film I had never heard of. But taking a guess, I carried on.

"Did this film win an Oscar for best picture?" I asked.

"No," he laughed.

Getting a flashback to my own high school days, I recalled, "Eric, there was a cheesy banner that hung in my high school's library. It read, 'What is popular is not always right, what is right is not always popular.' Cheesy, I know. But there is some truth to that."

He laughed in his typical Eric fashion.

Over the next ten minutes we began to unpack this idea further. Most importantly, we began to explore the observation that by chasing after popular opinion, the creative process is stinted. It is difficult to pull together a cohesive project formed from a variety of ideas people like. The creative process takes authorship and not just mere collaging. Further, by seeking popular opinion too soon in the process, the project never has time to develop past the awkward phase into its eventual goodness. But most of all, by valuing affirmation from the crowd, you are less likely to take risks with the project.

Failure and the Creative Process

Although different in their approach, Emma and Eric both suffered from the ills of vainglory, causing their creativity to not flourish. By having an excessive desire for recognition and approval from others, it prevented them from the being able to risk failure and loose the approval. And since they were unable to risk failure, they were unable to carry out a fully flourishing creative process.

As scholars and practitioners of creativity attest, risk-taking and failure are key ingredients to a successful creative process. Over the past fifty years, researchers examining the relationship between creativity and risk, or failure, have consistently found that individuals who are willing to take on more risk, or risk failure, consistently produce more creative works.[12] These studies have shown that two things happen for people who are more willing to risk failure. First, they are willing to explore, and give merit, to the exploration of unconventional ideas. And by being willing to seriously consider these ideas, novel, high quality, and useful works emerge. Second, people who are willing to risk failure simply find a freedom to try—and try more often. Thus, these people are not fundamentally more creative—per say—but simply take more shots at the goal. And if you take more shots at the goal, the number of successful scores simply increases.

To let creativity flourish, you must be able to risk failing. But if our natural desire for acknowledgment is out of balance, we are unable to successfully risk that failure. After speaking with a thousand individuals to explore the role that insecurity plays in a person's life, scholar Brené Brown observed, "When our self-worth isn't on the line, we are far more willing to be courageous and risk sharing our talents and gifts."[13] And thus if we keep our desire for affirmation in balance, we are able to perform "risk taking and trailblazing inherent in creative endeavors."[14]

If we cannot risk failure, we cannot flourish in our creativity. If we have an excessive and disordered desire for approval from others, we cannot flourish in our creativity. Emma's ambition made her excessively seek the recognition of those with creative authority—from professors to internships to critics in design magazines. Eric's vainglory sought applause and acknowledgment from the largest number of people possible. And because of this, neither of them were able to risk the potential of losing this approval through failure. And because of this, neither of them flourished in their creativity.

---

12. See Atkinson, *Introduction to Motivation*; Cropley, "Fostering Creativity in the Classroom," 83–114; Perkins, *Mind's Best Work*; Shekerjian, *Uncommon Genius*; Sternberg and Lubart, *Defying the Crowd*.

13. As quoted in Kelley and Kelley, *Creative Confidence*, 57.

14. Kelley and Kelley, *Creative Confidence*, 57.

FREEDOM TO FAIL

Vainglory is a twisted branch in our tree, choking off flourishing fruit of creativity. To begin to find freedom from a disordered need for acknowledgment, we must start by pruning the branch.

Pruning is never an easy task. Like any vice, the branch is the resulting buildup of long-practiced habits; the habits of chasing false glory. These habits have subsequently created thick layers, rendering the branch resistant to pruning. Therefore, any attempt to remove the branch, and its ill fruit, will take great intentionality, consistent reworking of habits, and the work of a master Arborist. To simply look in the mirror and say, "I'm going to change today," will not make even a small nick in the branch. Vice laden habits must be intentionally replaced with habits leading to the good.[15] Although these new patterns will feel awkward at first, it is through consistent practice that new ruts in the road are cut. Finally, when the new ruts find their depth, these actions come with ease and our instincts have changed. But none of this is possible without the master Arborist.[16] As thousands of years of individuals seeking to remove vice from their life have attested, without submitting your vice to the Lord, and seeking his grace, efforts are futile.

The vice of vainglory is a vice of excess desire. Consequently, the disciplines used to inform new habits are disciplines of restraint and denial. The spiritual disciplines begin with a longer period of restraint with the intent to bring awareness to the ingrained excess desire. Following, these longer periods can be transferred to smaller habitual practices. The applied disciplines for vainglory include the practices of silence and secrecy.[17]

Silence

Vainglory, and its quest for false glory, is often manifested in our words. We exaggerate, make up stories, highlight our accomplishments, and bring ourselves to the center of attention—all in hopes of receiving acknowledgment. Therefore, the first discipline is silence. Now this certainly does not mean that we shouldn't ever talk. Rather, in the case of vainglory, the discipline

---

15. Aquinas, *Summa Theologica*, ST I-II, q. 49, a.4.

16. Eph 2:1–10; 1 John 1–9.

17. Calhoun, *Spiritual Disciplines Handbook*, 104, 107.

of silence seeks to stop the spin we put on our lives.[18] In silence we seek to stop manipulating conversation to put the spotlight on ourselves—relying only on our actions to stand witness.

24 Hour Challenge: Because of the habitual nature of vices, we are unaware of just how prevalent they are in our daily interactions. So the first step is to practice silence from the spin for an extended period of time. One effective initial practice, suggested by Dr. DeYoung, an expert on vainglory, is to attempt to not speak about yourself, share your side of the story, or offer accounts of our own feelings for a twenty-four-hour period. As she writes,

> Would it be difficult, for a single day, to let our actions speak for themselves, without defending ourselves when we suspect others are being critical? . . . Could we listen to others, while refraining from conversation about ourselves—without telling stories about ourselves, recounting our own versions of events, or offering an account of our own feelings?[19]

After attempting to do this for twenty-four hours, reflect on just how difficult this exercise was. Take note of how often you had to fight back the urge to bring yourself into the center of the conversation. Recognize that your urge to center on yourself prevented you from listening to other individuals. Explore whether the discipline got easier with practice as time went on.

Highlighting Others: In seeking undue acknowledgment we can steal glory from others. To reverse this habit, we need to build an instinct to highlight others over ourselves. Make it a point once per day to initiate a conversation with others that brings other people's goodness into the spotlight—making sure it is a bright spotlight. Comment on the person's admirable qualities, successful creative ideas, and acknowledge how this has affected or inspired you. This can be done directly to the person, or more effectively in a larger group.

Now, there are caveats to this practice. Correcting vainglory is a process of removing the excess and applying due glory. So in highlighting others, this cannot tip into flattery—or excessive undue praise. Nor can it tip into giving glory for vain or unworthy acts. Interestingly, we tend to have a more calibrated gauge of how-much-is-too-much when we provide

18. Foster, *Freedom of Simplicity*, 94–109.

19. DeYoung, *Glittering Vices*, 75.

acknowledgment than when we seek it for ourselves. Our vainglory demands more applause than we are comfortable giving to others. Thus, this practice is effective in silencing your attempts to seek glory. Additionally, this practice works to recalibrate your gauge for how much, and for what things, acknowledgment is due.

Failure Portfolio: The strong hold of vainglory, as we have seen in this chapter, often prevents us from failing. We are either unwilling or unable to potentially sacrifice the applause for the sake of risking further creative development. To rework this pattern, this discipline seeks to flip the script. In a vainglorious pattern, successes are highlighted and failures are hidden. Reverse it. Keep your creative successes silent, and highlight your creative failures. To do so, construct a failure portfolio which showcases your creative process failures.

In the portfolio, collect images or other artifacts that document the failure and review them for their sources and potential lessons. Categorize each failure into one of four failure categories:[20]

1) Skill: Skill failures occur when your technical skill set is underdeveloped such that you are not able to bring an idea you have in mind to fruition.

2) Concept: Concept failures occur when the root idea for a creative project loses its persuasion, or ordering ability, once you begin to examine the idea during creative development.

3) Judgment: Judgment failures can come from a multitude of directions including wrong judgment on your part to add to or edit your work; your willingness to let someone else's judgment unduly shape the project; or incorrect judgment by all parties on the needs and constraints for the project's output.

4) Nerve: Nerve failures occur when you do not try to develop a great idea due to lack of confidence or fear of failing in others' eyes.

Once completed, show others your failure portfolio with pride. Highlight your failures and speak nothing of the eventual success. Give yourself credit for failing. With this discipline, failure becomes normalized, success gets rightsized, and vainglory begins to be pruned.

---

20. For further discussion on the following categories, as well as additional categories of failure, see Tharp, *Creative Habit*, 215–16.

Secrecy

The vice of vainglory warps our motivations. When we have the twisted branch of vainglory, acts of goodness, truth, or beauty are done in hopes of receiving applause. These acts are no longer done simply because they are good, true, or beautiful. Donating creative services to an organization is no longer about doing good, but about the potential for marketing and further recognition. An initial impulse to create a new product to help an ailing brother becomes the compelling origin story that attracts investors. Friendly dinners meant to build community among small business owners becomes a strategic networking opportunity to build a name-dropping repertoire. And, creative works are made to impress instead of bring goodness, truth, and beauty into the world.

Therefore, the discipline of secrecy works to instill habits that guard these motivations. By valuing secrecy,[21] we can free ourselves from the temptation to twist creation into applause.

Quiet Success: A person who has the character trait of vainglory wants people to know how successful they are. Changing this habit comes in small steps. Prior to the weekend, reflect on the successes of the week. Choose one key success and intentionally choose not to share it with anyone over the weekend. After the weekend is over, reflect on your ability to accomplish this, and challenges you faced.

Keeping success a secret, as a means to prune vainglory, is a challenge in both the act and the achievement of the act. Ironically, not telling about your week's success is often not the most difficult part. The most difficult part is not telling someone that you were successful in not telling someone. Or in other words, come Monday, the urge to share your small triumph over vainglory will often be stronger than your initial urge to share your week's accomplishment. It is important to discipline this urge, and keep both levels of success a secret for five days following.

The Solo Exhibit: Making creative works is accomplished most successfully through a collaborative process. However, when vainglory is existent, collaborators become audiences. Thus, this discipline is a temporary exercise to begin reforming motives. Identify a smaller creative idea that you have had in mind. Begin to develop this idea, without telling anyone, and

---

21. Jesus valued secrecy, telling people on more than one occasion not to tell others about the good things they did. See Matt 6:3–4.

without showing anyone. Continue to develop the idea through its failures and successes. Bring the project into full completion and presentation quality. When it is done, keep is solely to yourself.

Now, it is natural to think, "This is some of my best work, it is important to bring it to the light." Resist this urge, and reflect on the satisfaction of simply developing a creative work solely for its goodness, truth, or beauty. Consciously try to replace the need for applause with the gratification of producing the creative act.

All the disciplines above will be hard and feel unnatural. Anytime habits are broken and instincts are denied it feels unnatural. Vainglory creates an almost unquenchable craving for applause. So when we work to deny the applause, we feel empty and deprived. But as anyone who has attempted to reduce the amount of food they eat can testify, eventually the stomach feels as if it "shrinks." After a short period of time, two slices of pizza renders us full whereas a month previous, the entire pizza would be required. The same with vainglory. We will have hunger pangs, and never feel full. But with intentionality, and partnership with God, our desires will "shrink" to a balanced level. And once we are balanced, we are able to more freely fail, and more freely able to flourish in our creativity.

• • •

All of humanity has a natural appetite to please other human beings and a desire to be acknowledged. We should seek to employ creativity in the process of pleasing other humans. We should be acknowledged for our creative acts. It is good.

But as Emma and Eric experienced, when creativity is slave to applause, it cannot flourish; it does not produce good fruit. Vainglory must be pruned from our character to allow creativity to flourish.

3

Envy

BY THE TIME STUDENTS reach university education, they are well versed in the rhythms of schoolwork. For twelve plus years, students are taken through innumerable academic exercises which have very detailed and precise instructions for completion. Starting in elementary school, students are given a worksheet with a diagram that supports the day's lesson. On the top of the worksheet there are clear instructions to color the diagram using the colors indicated by the numbers in the key; and so they do.

In middle school students are welcomed into scientific laboratory-based classrooms for hands-on instruction. The scientific laboratory is one of the most creative spaces in our contemporary culture; unfortunately, students do not participate in this way. Paired up with a lab partner, students are handed an instruction sheet with step-by-step instructions for the experiment. The only inventive work is a self-reflection at the end of the experiment.

In high school, students are given slightly more freedom, but still within strong parameters. In English class students are provided the opportunity to choose a topic to write a research report on—provided it comes from a preapproved list. Following, students are set loose to develop the paper, as long as it remains within a three-part argument structure with two subpoints each, is formatted to a certain standard, and falls between 1,000 and 1,100 words.

From elementary school through high school graduation, students learn that the key to academic success is the ability to carefully follow instructions. So when these very same students enroll in a university course on creativity, they experience a bit of a shock to the system. Thus when students are faced with ambiguity, creative freedom, and little to no clarification instead of precise instructions, emotions arise. They feel disoriented, frustrated, and mislead.

Having taught courses on creativity for many years, I have come to expect, and welcome, these reactions. It is through this process that students begin to learn firsthand the rhythms of a self-driven creative process. With this aim in mind, one of the first assignments given in the creativity course is intentionally designed to have students experience this transition in an overt way. In this assignment, students are given the assignment to produce fifty works in a week's time. Period. No more instruction; no clarifications; no real limitations except that it cannot be one work cut up into fifty pieces. Students' reactions to this assignment express the full range of emotions—and the spring session that Sarah was enrolled in was no different.

After I gave the short brief of the assignment, pairs of eyes stared blankly back at me—awaiting more information. So when I started to move onto the next topic of the day, nearly every hand in the room quickly shot up in the air.

"Professor, what is a work?" asked on student.

"Good question," I replied, and called on another student.

"Does it have to be a work of art—like painting?" she asked.

"That will be interesting to explore." I called on another student in the back.

"How big does it have to be?" He asked.

I smiled and answered, "Yes," and called on another student. I could sense the growing frustration in the room, as well as the student's realization that there really was not going to be more clarification. As the prodding of the definition of work slowed down, reality of the assignment sunk in.

"Professor, I think I may have misheard you say fifty. What is the actual number due?" a student asked in a persuasive tone.

"Thank you for asking. Yes, I did say fifty—due one week from today," I confirmed.

After ten minutes of inquiry and rebuff, nearly every student had taken a stab at getting more information—all but Sarah.

Sarah sat in the second-to-back row of desks. She was quiet, but not in a way that was unapproachable. The few times that she looked up from her notebook, she gave a casual smile to anyone looking—then quickly retreated back into her doodles. Even as all the commotion of the 50 Works assignment ensued around her, she remained calm and engrossed in her notebook. At no time during that class session did Sarah raise her hand.

Although it is often normal for a student to not participate early in the class, I always want to make sure that any student feels comfortable to talk in class. Unsure of whether Sarah was just shy or she felt uncomfortable jumping in, I attempted to make eye contact with her, giving unspoken permission to speak—to no avail.

Class continued on for another twenty minutes. When the bell rang indicating the end of class, the clock officially started for the "works" creation. As I was packing up my things, I glanced up and noticed that despite the growing buzz of students discussing the project further, Sarah still wasn't engaging. As she walked past my desk, I asked, "Sarah, everything okay? You ready for this assignment?"

"Oh yes, Professor, I am actually looking forward to it. Thanks for asking." She gave a quick small smile and continued out the room.

One week never feels as short as when you are assigned to create fifty works. Before the students knew it, the fifty works were due. I tend to arrive to class quite early the day the fifty works are due knowing students come in with wagons full of works, requiring me to play traffic cop to keep things orderly. On this particular day, when I arrived, I opened the door expecting an empty room. Instead, I saw one student already preparing. Sarah was sitting in the second-to-back row, with her works spread in front of her. She was carefully arranging and rearranging her works. The care she was putting into her small display showed the level of pride she had in her creative products. I was pleased by her thoughtfulness and glad to see her excitement.

Shortly after my arrival, the rest of the students began to arrive, works in tow. The room filled with a vast array of colors, materials, and artifacts. Students darted back and forth looking at what other students had come up with. From one side of the room, a group of students burst into laughter. The other side, expressions of admiration rose up. As the noise reached peak level, I called the students to order.

As the class session progressed, student after student stood up to say a few words about what they experienced that week, and describe their final products. We had worked our way through the first two rows, and were about to start on the second-to-back row, when I glanced in Sarah's direction. To my surprise, there was nothing in front of her. Where there had been a carefully arranged set of works, now sat one small pile—faced upside down. She had stacked all of her works, and placed them out of view from anyone.

When it was Sarah's turn, I asked, "Sarah, would you like to share?"

She sat quietly, looking down at her doodle notebook. After about twenty seconds of silence had passed, I noticed quiet tears where beginning to stream down her face. Wanting to relieve her potential embarrassment, I offered that we come back to her. She nodded, and as I was about to call on the next person, she quietly said, "May I be excused?" I nodded. She picked up her notebook and quickly slipped out of the room.

I didn't see Sarah for the rest of the class period. It was only after all the other students had filed out and I was packing up my things that Sarah reentered the class. Looking cautiously at her, I asked, "Sarah, is everything okay?"

With clear sadness and frustration she kept her head down, and quietly answered, "I just couldn't show my work. Everybody's work was just so much better than mine. Why can't I be as creative as them? Why can't I produce works like them? I'm just really frustrated."

I tried to reassure her, but to no avail. Sarah could not stop focusing on other peoples' works long enough to see the potential in her own. Even in these short few minutes her emotions moved from sadness to anger, and back again. As she left the room, I encouraged her to try to stay focused on her creative development, and not be distracted by others.

But as the semester would prove out, this was not possible for Sarah. She only became more obsessed with other peoples' works, and consequently failed to develop her own creativity in a meaningful way.

Sarah's creativity was held captive to the *vice of envy*.

THE VICE OF ENVY

Sarah's actions and words could possibly be described by a number of related vices: envy, covetousness, or jealousy. In contemporary culture, we use these terms synonymously. However, there are key differences between these vices, and each have fundamentally different manifestations. As Sarah's story will prove out, she truly suffered from debilitating envy. But prior to telling Sarah's full tale, it is important that we briefly explore what envy is, and how it differs from covetousness and jealousy.[1]

1. For a lengthier discussion, see DeYoung, *Glittering Vices*, 42–44.

In a general sense, we tend to mix these terms because we have a sense they all share a basic powerful urge to have something we do not. Furthermore, we tend to indiscriminately use these terms on account of the shared stomach-gnawing feeling they produce. But, envy, jealousy, and covetousness all derive from a different set of conditions and motivations.

To begin, we can categorize jealousy into a "have" category, and covetousness and envy into a "have-not" category.[2] Unlike envy or covetousness, jealousy has the object of desire. However, jealousy deeply fears losing it. Whether "it" is a relationship, position of influence, or a child's doll, to see another begin to infringe upon the thing we love gnaws at our stomachs. We become jealous when our girlfriend innocently participates in a study group with a male friend. In such a case, we fear that the love we have for the person will be taken away by her friend. Or from the eyes of a three-year-old, we scream and yell when another child takes a favorite toy. We fear that the other child will steal the toy we love forever. In short, jealousy loves loving something or someone so much we seek to unduly possess it for our own; wrenching and screaming if the love is threatened.

Envy and covetousness are different. In both of these vices, we get a knot in our stomach because we do not have the thing we desire. To covet something is to want something someone else has. In particular, when we covet, we want that exact thing. Let's return to our three-year-old. A child will often become despondent when he wants a red ball that another child has. A greedy child would simply want to have a ball too, and perhaps several balls just to add to his collection. But a covetous child isn't satisfied with any ball, or ten balls for that matter. He must have the red ball the other kid is holding. It doesn't matter that the adult tries to hand him a yellow ball to play with; he must have the red one. The tears and screaming will not stop until he has that exact ball. So for covetousness, the key desire is to possess the exact something another individual has.

Envy shares some similar characteristics to covetousness, but is rooted in much more malicious motivations. Similar to someone who covets, an envious person too wants the exact something another individual has. However, envy gets just as much pleasure from seeing the other person not have the thing anymore, as having the thing itself.

If we return to our three-year-old's desire for the red ball, we can begin to see the mechanics of envy. Kicking and screaming accompany the child's desire to have the other kid's red ball; yellow balls nor ten red balls will

2. DeYoung, *Glittering Vices*, 44.

suffice. But when the adult persuades the child with the red ball to share, our envious three-year-old will smile, take the ball, drop it, and begin to play with something else. Yes, it was about the particular red ball. But it was just as much about the redistribution of the ball, and the equaling out of the child's status with a rival.

Although the example of a three-year-old helps illustrate the manifestation of envy, there are some very real and very adult emotions that undergird this vice. Fundamentally, envy despises the life God has given, and longs for a life that God has given someone else. In most cases, envy is not about a ball. Envy primarily yearns for the qualities of another person—including talents or status. And in doing so, envy places self-worth up for comparison with others, fostering feelings of low self-worth. It is from this state of perceived low worth that envy creates a self-perpetuating future.

When an envious person stews in desire for another person's qualities, they silently admit that their qualities are inferior. Thus, an envious person typically will not overtly take any action to obtain such admirable qualities. They will never ask the other individual for help, or seek to bring themselves up to the same level. The preference is to destroy the other, rather than build oneself up. Envy is not productive, it is destructive.

Thus, envy starts to manifest in ways that aim to destroy the other. Granted, these attempts are not from a full frontal attack, believing itself inferior. Rather envy seeks to destroy the other through coy, underhanded, passive-aggressive tactics. Gossip, belittling, backbiting, antagonism, and snickering are all tools in the envy toolbox.[3] Most often, these do nothing to the admirable qualities of the other. Instead they simply work to dig envy deeper into the individual, eating at the person more and more.

As awful as these are, we pray that envy goes no farther beyond passive-aggressive attacks. Unfortunately this is not always the case; envy is a formidable foe if allowed to fester. Envy, at times, can possess a person to such an extent that it finds a partnership with the vice of wrath, and quickly moves from passive-aggressive to aggressive—rendering the admired individual in harm's way.

Fortunately for Sarah, and for the other students in my creativity class, her envy did not root this deeply. But unfortunately for Sarah, it did render its destructive tendencies in her life—and her notebook was testimony to the agony.

---

3. DeYoung, *Glittering Vices*, 45–47.

As part of the requirements of the creativity course, students are asked to keep a notebook for sketches, design ideas, and general creative development. I make it clear that these are not personal journals and that we will collect and evaluate them on a periodic basis. So I was taken a bit aback when the day I first collected the notebooks, the typically quiet Sarah spoke up and asked, "Do I have to turn mine in?" I nodded, confirming that if she wanted a grade, she needed to submit her notebook for evaluation. She quietly obliged.

Later that week when I sat down to evaluate the notebooks I discovered why Sarah was hesitant. As I observed in the first few weeks of class, Sarah often doodled in her notebook. Small drawings in the margins filled the book. I may have overlooked them if I didn't notice one particular drawing.

In this drawing, Sarah had drawn a sketch of the 50 Works assignment presentations. She had drawn one of her classmates presenting with word bubbles, "These are my 50 works. Aren't they amazing?" The rest of the class was drawn as a crowd with the word bubbles, "You are so creative." But the next frame of the storyboard changed tone quickly.

In the next frame, this same student was pictured walking in the cafeteria, holding a tray of food. With amazing technical ability, the drawing then showed this individual tripping and landing face first in a pile of food. A character wearing a "Sarah" T-shirt stood by laughing with the word bubble, "How creative are you now?"

Unfortunately, this was one of many, many drawings. As the notebook progressed, the pictures became more frequent. These doodles were a manifestation of Sarah's envy. She longed to have the creative abilities of her classmates. And instead of working harder to increase her skills, the poison of envy slowly poisoned her focus to a point of obsessing over how good her class was compared to her. Sarah's longing to be creative was overshadowed by her longing to be her classmates—or at least see them smash their face in a pile of food.

Sarah was clearly ensnared by envy. Unsure if I could help, but feeling like someone needed to extend a hand, I asked her to join me for office hours the next week.

ENVY AND EXPRESSIVE INDIVIDUALISM

The next week, Sarah showed up to my office at the prescribed time. She quietly moved into the chair across from my desk, silently placed her bag down, and without hesitation asked in a forthright by shy tone, "Is this about the notebook?"

"Yes, Sarah, it is. I'm sure you have a sense of why I wanted to talk with you today. I want to make sure you are okay—the doodles in your notebook seem to indicate that you may be struggling a bit. Is there anything you want to talk about?" I asked.

"I don't know, Professor. Why can't I be as creative as my classmates?" she lamented.

"Sarah, I think you have great creative potential. I saw how proud you were of your fifty works when I came into the room. And you should have been proud. You put a lot of effort into the assignment, and your work showed real promise and quality craftsmanship," I encouraged.

With her eyes fixed on her lap she mumbled, "You are just saying that because you have to."

"Let me assure you, I'm not. Just like all your other classmates, you are beginning your creative development—and you started well at the beginning. Can I ask, why do you feel you are not as creative?" I asked cautiously.

Sarah responded, "I can't do the things they do. I don't know how to use digital tools, and I can't draw as well as them. All the stuff they produce looks better than mine."

Not wanting her to spiral too deep, I interjected, "Sarah, these are all technical skills you too can learn. Each student in class has had to learn these. Most students are actively working to better these skills."

Pausing to see if I could get her to acknowledge, without avail, I continued, "As a matter of fact, I think there are two or three study groups that get together on a weekly basis to go over technical tutorials, and learn from each other. One student told me they regularly rotate to share tips and tricks they find to be useful. If you would like I can introduce you to the leaders—they are very welcoming."

Sarah sat, staring out the window onto the university lawn. We simply sat in the silence for two to three minutes. Finally she looked up and said, "I don't think that will help."

"May I ask why?" I inquired.

"If I'm in a study group, we are all learning the same thing. We all get better together," she said.

Curious, I asked, "Isn't that the goal? All of us participating in this creativity course, collectively aim to refine our creativity. I would hope that at the end of this experience, we could consider ourselves a creative community, all having developed our creative skills."

She shot back, seemingly a bit frustrated, "Life just doesn't work that way. There are only a certain amount of high grades in a class. There are only a certain amount of desirable jobs out there. Not everybody can be successful. We all can't be the best. At the end of the day, there are winners and losers in the game of life. I must look after myself. I have to succeed."

Taking a breath, she continued, "I can see a model of success, what it takes, and who that type of person is. And unfortunately, right now it is not me—it is the talented students in my class. That's the model. That is what I need to become. And when I become just like them, I will have the best chance to succeed."

The conversation lasted for about twenty more minutes. With each conversational volley, I attempted to encourage Sarah in her creativity, and extol her to participate in the group's success. Unfortunately, Sarah fundamentally viewed herself as an individual—and unfortunately an individual that was inferior to the "model" of creative success demonstrated by her fellow students. Sarah was living the reality of desiring success in a culture dominated by expressive individualism.

As we have previously unpacked, expressive individualism places an emphasis on a person's ability to manifest their uniqueness. Individuals who are able to successfully do this become the definition of a well-lived authentic life. Yet, as we have also previously seen, to do this, one must deny any external source of self-meaning. This includes meaning derived from dutiful participation in religion, institutions, and communities.

Prior to the rise of the "be true to yourself" movement, the way an individual lived a meaningful life was by contentedly fulfilling their role within a community.[4] If your family served as the village shoemaker, there was an expectation that you would take up your family trade and become the next generation of shoemakers. This was the role that your family played in the larger needs of the community. Your identity wasn't rooted in the fact you were a shoemaker, but it was grounded by knowing you were playing your part in making a successful community. If you didn't make the shoes, no one would. The community needed you, and you willingly played your part. Community tied together purpose and meaning for an individual.

However, a community focused purely on identity, while able to provide meaning, did also have the ability to suppress an individual's God-given

---

4. Taylor, *Ethics of Authenticity*, 2–4.

talent if it was not aligned with the family business. Not all shoemakers gave birth to talented shoemakers, sometimes a father's son was different than himself. Christian teaching thus emphasizes the notion of vocation. Or in other words, Christianity teaches that God created each individual with specific talents for a specific purpose in bringing God glory and loving their neighbors effectively. Therefore, a central aim of life, and source of identity, is the act of living out one's vocation in service of community, honoring God in the process. Christian teaching of vocation relocates identity from a binding community requirement to a focus on God and his call to serve—even if that means not becoming a shoemaker.

Yet, for some, freedom found in God was not enough freedom. For complete freedom, as systems of thought like expressive individualism purport, one must only look to internal passions, denying community and any God-given expectations for their life. Accordingly, expressive individualism places a strong emphasis on "individual." Standing in opposition to a community-rooted life, an expressive individualist denies community and external expectations in order to cater to individual passions freely. If the community needs you to be a shoemaker, but your passion is cooking, the right thing to do would be to abandon shoemaking; to be a shoemaker would be a travesty.[5] You should leave your community in order to chase your dream of working with food. Meaning comes from attending to your inner desire—despite any community needs found in family, politics, township, or even religion.

Thus, the picture of a culture influenced by expressive individualism is not a picture of community, or individuals seeking to love God and love neighbors well.[6] Rather, it is a picture of individual atoms floating near and by each other; each pursuing their own goals, attempting to not get in the way of other atoms doing the same.[7] A "be true to yourself" motto highlights the individual, but also advocates that the highest ethic requires that we do not deny others their ability to chase their passions. Thus, at the end of the day, everyone can seek their passion and live a fulfilling life. A very nice system, in theory.

But as Sarah pointed out, life doesn't always work out that way. Sometimes atoms bump into each other as they seek to occupy the same space. Even if one's aim is to live out a passion, in reality, to some extent, not

---

5. Taylor, *Ethics of Authenticity*, 15–17.

6. Keller, *Preaching*, 131; 140–45.

7. Taylor, *Ethics of Authenticity*, 95–100.

everybody can succeed in this quest. No matter how much someone wants to be a professional athlete, there are only so many slots on the roster. No matter how much I chase my dream, I may not be allotted the opportunity to play professional sports for money. No matter how much I desire to lead in government, I may not be voted in as a senator. No matter how much I dream to be a research scientist, I may not have the aptitude for detailed research. Same goes for becoming a top chef or professor or designer who receives the best commissions. A system that prioritizes the individual over community within an organically competitive structure of success will eventually deny someone's passion. With ultimate meaning riding on one's ability to live out their passion, there is a lot at stake. And where there is a lot at stake, fierce competition ensues.

In a community-based system, individuals are able to rejoice for the success of someone in the community. Their success means my success. But in a competitive individualistic system, we cannot cheer for others authentically. When someone else succeeds, I do not. Thus, instead of learning and sharing within a community structure, we aggressively compare ourselves to others; wishing that we were like those that are succeeding. Or in other words, expressive individualism will tend to see the world through competitive goggles; rendering an individual vulnerable to the vice of envy; a vulnerability Sarah fell to.

Sarah was unwilling to celebrate the success of her classmates, nor join them in collective learning. By doing so, she believed there was a chance she may not be able to fully succeed in her passions. Ironically—but not surprisingly—it was those students who did fully participate in the community that advanced the most in their creative skills. Sarah, in seeking to be true to herself, self-selected out of community, opting for individual success. With individualistic glasses on, the answer to lack of success for Sarah was not to join community, but rather to become a different individual.

ENVY AND CREATIVITY

Over the course of the semester, I unfortunately watched Sarah sink deeper and deeper into the desire to be a different creative individual. She slowly transitioned from initial pride in her 50 Works projects, to mere imitation of other students' work. At one point in the semester, she became so obsessed with another student's style, that the final submission was so similar it triggered a plagiarism inquiry. Sarah was so envious of other students' "successful" creativity, she upheld their creative qualities as the exact mold for achieving flourishing creativity. Unfortunately, by seeking such an exact mold, her creativity became disordered.

The wonderful part about creativity is that it produces novel works that bring to the world a new level of understanding goodness, truth, or beauty. Granted, the novelty of a creative work is never fully original. No one, besides God the creator, creates something completely new out of nothing. The act of creativity is an act of mixing and remixing elements and ideas available to us. Therefore, within any creative process, inspiration is foundational. Any flourishing creative process sees and studies life around them—including other creative works. With these sources of inspiration and knowledge as foundational building blocks, an individual's creative process uniquely creates something that is novel, of high quality, and appropriately useful. Undergirding this successful creative process are two central principles—both of which Sarah's envy prevented her from understanding.

First, a flourishing creative process does not begin with a fully-worked-out end in mind. The creative process is one of discovery, experimentation, and development—all of which are fueled from foundational inspiration. As soon as the creative process replaces discovery with the desire to produce a creative work just like X, inspiration becomes imitation. And, as one can easily imagine, a process fueled by imitation is a disordered creative process which ceases to produce novel works.

When Sarah's envious desire fixated on other students' creative works, the healthy process of inspiration morphed into a creatively unhealthy longing to imitate. Her idea of success was a predetermined mold; she needed to be just like another student. And by doing so, she gave up her ability to reformulate elements around her in a uniquely creative way. By imitating other students, her works were no longer novel, and thus no longer creative.

Second—one level deeper—because a flourishing creative process does not begin with a fully-worked-out end in mind, a successful creative process requires the creator to be content with ambiguity. Unlike simple math or language grammar, most often, there is no single correct answer to a creative problem. Granted, there are more fitted and appropriate creative solutions than others. In attempting to go to the moon, we could creatively suggest we stack wheels of cheese, and climb to the moon. Yes, this is a unique idea, but it is not the most fitted, or successful, creative idea compared to the idea of using propulsion to launch a space vehicle through the atmosphere. But even so, the typical creative process does not work within an existing framework fully guiding one's decisions and actions.[8] A creative process requires ambiguity.

Scholars and researchers have observed the key role that ambiguity plays in creativity. A successful creative, research has shown, is one that is comfortable with an ambiguous process.[9] Successful creatives remain open, and often find joy, in a process where there is no overt procedure, not all facts are known, and questions are discovered along the way.[10] And because there are no set expectations or procedures, creatives are more able to "think outside the box." Or in other words, successful creatives do not assume there are rules to follow when things are ambiguous—allowing them to discover novel solutions.[11] Creativity requires a contentment with ambiguity; and the willingness to see it through to the final discovery of a novel, high-quality, and useful final work.

Unfortunately the vice of envy strips this contentment away. Envy makes us discontent with ourselves, and thus, untrusting of our ability to navigate through ambiguity. We see other creative individuals producing work that we deem better than our own. We fixate on the final creative product, wanting to produce something just like it—wanting to be like its creator. And in doing so, we apply a set of rules onto our creativity; forcing ourselves to stay within a predetermined box. Sarah's creativity became disordered the minute her creativity aimed to be just like X. She needed to know that the final creative product would be like X and thus achieve success. Ironically, though, her desire to produce just like X robbed her of the very quality that made her classmates creatively successful—contentment with ambiguity. Envy stripped her of this contentment, and thus stripped her of a flourishing creativity.

CREATIVE CONTENTMENT

Of all the vices, envy is notably the most torturous of vices. Other vices offer a false promise of something good, such as pleasure, praise, wealth, or escape before leading into misery. Envy has no such enticement; it goes

8. Dacey et al., *Understanding Creativity*, 98.

9. Jay and Perkins, "Problem Finding," 257–93; Sarnoff and Cole, "Creative and Personal Growth," 95–102.

10. MacKinnon, *In Search of Human Effectiveness*, 324–25.

11. Getzels, "Creativity: Process and Issues," 326–44; Torrance, *Search for Satori*.

straight to misery through "sorrow over another's good."[12] Through envy's evil eye, the world becomes a competition; one in which we are unsuited to win. Therefore, every time we see a friend or companion succeed, we feel as if we are being called into question. The very act of their success belittles us. And in return we burn with the desire to level the playing field by belittling them. Envy works within a vicious formula: "dejection plus disparagement plus destruction."[13] We don't want them to be, because we want to be them.

Envy's malicious formula not only burns our stomachs, but creates bad patterns in our lives; the amplification of competition separates us from community, and the intense focus on inferiority stalls our recognition of goods in our lives which we can build on. Therefore, as we seek to prune the mean thorns of envy, we must seek to practice opposing but virtuous habits. The applied disciplines for envy include participation in community[14] and practice of contentment.

Community

Envy entices us to see the world as purely competitive; my rival's success or mine. Such a viewpoint will result in individualistic isolation. Our desire to have the qualities of another person will eventually separate us from community. Therefore, as we seek to loosen the grip of envy on our lives, we must intentionally seek to change these isolating patterns. To do so, we must seek out community in order to invest ourselves "deliberately and deeply in activities with shared or common goods."[15]

By participating in community where one person's engagement with the common good does not diminish anyone else's ability to enjoy the good, we can begin to experience the joy of shared experience and identity.[16] With enough intentional participation, community can "teach us how it feels to rejoice in something good," and as importantly, teach us to "rejoice in that good as shared with others."[17] Then, slowly, the desire for the pleasure that comes with shared joy will hopefully become more enticing than the desire for displeasure over another's success.

12. Aquinas, *ST* II-II q.36 a.1.1.

13. Guinness, *The Call*, 176.

14. Calhoun, *Spiritual Disciplines Handbook*, 129–31.

15. DeYoung, *Glittering Vices*, 55.

16. DeYoung, *Glittering Vices*, 55.

17. DeYoung, *Glittering Vices*, 55.

Noncompetitive Community Outing: To start the process of relearning how to experience shared joy, this exercise seeks to experience noncompetitive community activities. For this exercise, identify or form a community with eight to fifteen individuals; a community of this size requires full participation, but is not so small that one person can overshadow others. Plan an event for the community, ensuring the activity is noncompetitive and focuses on a common good. Examples of noncompetitive events include jointly experiencing goodness, truth, or beauty, such as experiencing a music performance together, taking a bike ride along a beautiful road, attending an interesting guest lecture, or even simply people watching and collectively identifying moments of goodness.

No matter the activity, the goal is to share noncompetitive joy in a community setting. At first, when used to envious life patterns, this will feel unnatural. Take some time after the gathering and reflect on the experience of sharing joy in community. Seek to intentionally compare these feelings with envious desires. Do note, one outing will not suffice to loosen envy's grip. But with continued participation in community, isolation will seem less attractive.

Learning Community; Creative Community: After seeking the joy in common goods, the next exercise is to experience communal joy centered on common goals. To do so, search out, or form, a learning community within your area of interest. Plan communal gatherings of four to seven individuals dedicated to learning a new skill or gaining a new level of understanding. Ensure that the steps taken to engage the interest are communal and shared. Do not distinguish between an instructor and learners; jointly discover and learn.

At first, the temptation will be to let competitive feelings slip in—becoming envious of an individual in the group who can pick up the material faster or with more skill. To guard against this, take time at the end of each group session to acknowledge each other's gains. Take turns celebrating another individual for their accomplishments, and identify how this makes the group better. Make sure everyone is acknowledged and that the primary focus is on the group's success. Following, discuss the goals for the next meeting—using the terms *we* and *our* as much as possible. For example, "Perhaps next week we can learn this new technique. Our skills will definitely improve from learning it." Continue with the group as long as feasible, reenforcing the ability to identify with and find joy in accomplishing communal goals.

Once the ability to experience joy in communal goals is achieved, the final step is to then begin to slowly attempt to be creative within the learning community. Find creative projects that require unique contributions from all members in the group. Ensure that the creative process is worked out during the community meetings only. Continue to use words like *we* and *our* over *I* and *my*. Start with smaller projects. Once completed, take intentional time to celebrate as a group the creative process and creative outcome; acknowledging within yourself the joy of creative participation.

Contentment

Envy is grounded in discontent. And from this discontent, envy produces two distinct emotional manifestations. First is a sense of inferiority with who we are compared to others. In this emotion, we reject the life we have for the lure of another's. Manifested in sadness, pity, and anger, this first set of emotions diminishes any goodness in one's creativity or creative works. The second emotion is encapsulated by the German word *schadenfreude*, or the delight found in the misfortune of others. This manifestation of discontent turns sadness for yourself into glee at the fall of your perceived superior.

In order to attend to the foundation of discontent, the virtue of contentment must be practiced. But in doing so, it is important to attend to both sides of the discontented emotions. Contentment exercises work to acknowledge existing honor within our lives as well as work to give due honor to "the superior other."

Revealing List: Envy strips us of the ability to recognize goodness, truth, and beauty within our creative lives and potentially within our future creative works. To rediscover these aspects, and fight feelings of discontented inferiority, carry out two different exercise within a notebook. First, focus on your creative process. At the start of a creative process write down five ways you hope the creative solution will further goodness, truth, or beauty in our world. Don't comment on what the final output will be, or what it will look like. Let the ambiguity of the final outcome remain ambiguous. Focus on the potential ways the product may contribute. Carry out the creative process, revisiting these five each week. In addition to reviewing these five ideas, each week add one more hope. At the end of the project go back and evaluate how many hopes were accomplished. Add more to the list if the outcome succeeds in different ways. Circle the successful hopes whose fulfillment surprised you the most. Take some time to feel contentment in the outcome, the process, and the ambiguity that led to it.

In the second part of this exercise, after feeling the contentment of the process, focus on a creative outcome. On a new sheet of the notebook, draw a vertical dividing line down the middle of the sheet. Now, select a similar creative work to yours that you admire. In one column write down ways you feel this admirable work succeeds in bringing goodness, truth, or beauty to the world. Stop at five entries. In the other column, repeat the exercise for your creative work. Ensure you record five entries. At this point, only add to the list if you add to your column first, making sure the lists are equal in length. Teach yourself to see the relative good in your work. Feel the contentment of your success; give due honor to your work.

Engage with the Enemy: In attempt to deal with discontentment, envy finds joy in striping due honor from the admired other. In doing so, it dehumanizes them so that their downfall is acceptable. To fight this envious habit, this exercise requires intentional engagement with the admired other. Of all the suggested exercises, this is the most difficult. Typically, envious individuals do not engage with the other on account of their sense of inferiority. So to directly engage is a fearful process. Thus, this exercise has two variants depending on the level of apprehension.

The first variant seeks to address the other directly. After identifying an appropriate time, and building the courage, go and speak to the "other"—another creative you are envious of. Start by simply introducing yourself. Then, in an attempt to restore due honor to them, tell them what you appreciate about their work. Finally, seek to re-humanize them in your mind by asking whether they would be willing to share some tips or tricks with you sometime. Take joy in your ability to engage and ask for help from someone you admire. See them as a resource and a human worthy of your honor.

If this proves too difficult at the start, the alternative variant of the exercise seeks to give them due honor through the act of praying for them. For the period of a week, to start, spend intentional time in prayer asking God to bless them, help them with their struggles, and endow confidence in their creativity. Furthermore, seek to thank God for the gifts he has given to this individual to bring goodness, truth, and beauty into the world. After some time, the act of praying for the individual will begin to re-humanize them and soften your desire to see harm come to them. Eventually you will begin to feel content with your position relative to theirs.

The intent of all the disciplines above is to reform the destructive habits of isolation and discontentment that envy breeds. Developing opposing habits of contentment and community will begin to reawaken your creativity and set it on its path to flourishing.

• • •

Envy squashes creative flourishing through undue competition which produces a sense of inferiority. And from this point of inferiority, we do not seek to improve our creativity, we instead become paralyzed, stewing in emotions of discontent.

Unfortunately, this web of discontent suffocated Sarah's creative process for the rest of the semester, and beyond. From my observation, Sarah was never able to shift her focus from simply becoming just like her classmates and seeking competitive success. Her obsession isolated her from seeking growth via community, and prevented her from experiencing contentment in the ambiguity of the creative process. Sarah eventually dropped out of the program, and in doing so, stopped pursuing her creative goals. Envy destroyed her strong creative potential; first disordering it—eventually destroying it. May her story stand as a warning to us all—creativity requires community and contentment in order to flourish.

4

Sloth

I WAS EMERGING INTO my third year of teaching as a young professor when my mentor stopped me in the hall and paid me what I thought was a touching compliment. With a smile he put his right hand on my shoulder in a fatherly way, and said, "You are becoming a good teacher." I smiled, grateful that this man, whom I looked up to, was affirming me—except he wasn't. He continued, "But you need to become six good teachers at the same time."

I paused, waiting for the Yoda-like wisdom to emerge from this backward statement.

After the distinct pause, he explained, "Within the creative fields, there are distinct creative personality types. You have honed your teaching well—but just for one type of student.. Open your eyes. See the other types of creative personalities. Learn to teach to them, too."

Just as quickly as he stopped me, he carried on his way—leaving me to stand there a bit perplexed. It wasn't until that following Wednesday when I saw James in studio, with his forehead on his desk, that I began to see what my mentor spoke of.

I had met James two semesters ago at the kick-off events for new students. By all first impressions, he had a natural intelligence and eagerness about him. As the year progressed, James set the bar high for his work ethic. He was always in the design lab, putting in the extra hours above and beyond his classmates. So when I walked into the design lab, the sight of him downtrodden was unexpected. Not wanting to pry on personal matters, but wanting to ensure he was okay, I made the statement, "I hope you are okay, James."

With a barely audible mumble, James said, "Professor, I don't know . . ."

Shooting his head straight up, revealing a face marked by indentations from his notebook, he lamented, "I don't know if I am cut out for this." His head slammed back down on the desk.

Sensing the need for a longer conversation, I found a nearby wall to lean on. Hoping to encourage him, I said, "James, you are the top of your class. And I bet you were the top of your class in high school, as well. You have a track record of succeeding when you put your mind to something. From what I've seen, you are doing great."

"But then why do I struggle?" James said, propping his cheek up on his hand.

"What do you mean? Your grades are doing well."

"I don't struggle with everything. Some of our creative exercises I love. But some of the exercises, and questions my professors ask—I just don't get," James reflected.

"What comes easy for you?" I inquired.

Without pause he perked up and started verbally processing, "I love the creative process—well, I think I do. I really enjoy taking a complex thing, with no end in sight, and finding a way through it. I love solving the puzzle. It's easy for me. When I look at the problem, I see its logic unfold in my mind. Once I see this, then it's easy to find the rational solution. I'm good at developing the strategy to solve the problem."

I responded, "Do you like strategy games, James?"

He responded, "I love playing strategy games, figuring out the game's rules, finding the loopholes, and succeeding despite them. And, I love winning in the end—but who doesn't? How did you know?"

"Just a hunch." I smiled.

Attempting to not get sidetracked into discussing hobbies, I prompted, "Sounds like a great creative skill set. So where do you feel like you struggle in your classes?"

"I struggle with the extra stuff. I solve the puzzle well—and most of my professors generally agree. But I just can never seem to answer a lot of the questions they ask. They don't make sense to me. Questions like: What does it feel like? How do you think people will engage with the solution? What would stop people from accepting the solution?"

James was growing more frustrated. He continued, "How will people engage with the solution? I don't know. . . . What does it feel like? I don't know. . . . But what I do know is that the solution works—I found the logic."

It was at this point in the conversation where my mentor's comments dawned on me. There are some creatives that are intuitively driven to look past conventional rules, and find novel solutions. These creatives rely on emotions to navigate the creative process, finding solutions that feel right—never thinking to ask, "Does it work?" This was not James.

James approached the creative process like a strategy game. Students like James are typically good at conventional schoolwork—loving math just as much as creativity. Their creative drive does not emerge from the need to express emotions, but is fueled by the nagging itch to answer the question, or to make something work better. For these students, creativity is not an extra exercise, but a natural—almost unreflective—means to an end. Understanding how people would feel, engage, or understand the solution is not a key consideration. Such considerations blur the logic, which dulls the resolution. For the Jameses of the world, the highest priority and deepest satisfaction is finding the ordered logic to solve the problem.

Reflecting on my conversation with James, my mentor's critique became clearer. Teaching creativity to these two different types of students required two very different approaches. Granted, I still don't know how my mentor figured there were six different creativity types—or if he himself knew. But his point was well taken.

James, and creatives like James, possess a unique set of giftings within the creative process. They are able to frame insightful questions to see the problem differently. They can identify underlying presuppositions and assumptions that others can't. They are able to develop incremental steps to eventually find a solution. And they are able to explain the process of reaching the solution well.

But like any strength, there exists an inherent propensity for weakness in other areas—which when habitually practiced can lead to moral vice. In James's case, he tended to put the problem over people. The hard work of empathetically considering people as a key variable in a creative solution was avoided. Creativity was an act of puzzle solving, and not an act of people loving. And the vice developed from these habits is known as *sloth*.

THE VICE OF SLOTH

Let me pause here to confirm that, yes, I meant to say "sloth." But let me also acknowledge your confusion.

In contemporary culture, when someone says the word sloth, the average person will mentally imagine a very slow, endearing, long-toed, furry creature that hangs upside down from a tree. This animal has become the mental picture for the contemporary understanding of this moral vice. This correlation is on account of its shared name, but also its shared characteristics. Just like the slow-moving animal, a person with the moral vice of sloth is thought of as a person whose character is defined by laziness.

Yet, from my description of James—the hardworking, successful student—you may say that the term "laziness" would not apply. And you would be correct. James was far from lazy. He worked harder, longer, and more resolutely than his peers. He was anything but lazy. But yet, according to the Christian tradition of moral formation, he still suffered from slothfulness.

As we seek to identify vice in our lives that hinders creative flourishing, it is important to have a nuanced understanding of the vices—lest we dismiss a symptom of our creative disorder. Sloth is laziness, but is not just laziness. To understand sloth, we must first say a few words about sloth's correlated virtue: diligence.

Diligence, by definition, describes careful and persistent work. At this level, it may seem that the term "laziness" is appropriately opposite. But diligence speaks about more than just finishing tasks, or checking off a to-do list. It is important to note that the Latin root of the word diligence is *diligere*, meaning "to love."[1] Yes, a diligent person—as we speak about it in contemporary culture—is a person who works on a task until it is done. But in the Christian tradition, a diligent person is someone who carefully and persistently attends to the demands of love. If someone loves something, they care deeply. And if they care deeply about it, their work reflects this care. A person who cares is a person who works conscientiously and persistently to tend to the love. Therefore the opposing vice, sloth, is the *apathy or resistance to the demands of love.*[2]

Friendship illustrates this principle well. Normally, the bonds of friendship are uplifting, joyful and fun. We share events and discussions

---

1. DeYoung, *Glittering Vices*, 81.
2. DeYoung, *Glittering Vices*, 79.

about life. We rely on them to encourage us when we are down. We laugh together until our faces hurt. But in any friendship, there are times when disagreements occur. Fights break out, hurtful words are spoken, and a fracture occurs. During these times, we don't feel like talking or seeing our friend. Rather, we dodge their calls and avoid seeing them. It is simply easier to not engage. It is precisely at this point, the point where it is simply easier to not engage, when sloth appears.

The right thing to do when there is a fracture in our relationship is to seek reconciliation or repentance. Because we love our friend, we should care enough to seek to mend the friendship. But this is hard work. Picking up the phone to call the friend is harder than simply pushing the call straight to voicemail. Intentionally going to visit our friend is harder than avoiding them. The demands of love are hard. So we avoid it; we become slothful.

Slothfulness manifests its avoidance to the demands of love in two different ways. In the first way, sloth is the image of a person sitting on the couch, not getting up—or moving slowly—to engage in the hard work. Or in other words, sloth is laziness. A person is lazy when they do not take the effort to mend their friendship by picking up the phone or visiting them. Instead they sit and watch a movie because it is easier; it is lazy. And repeated lazy habits toward love develops a slothful character. Slothfulness, in this version, is manifested through apathy.

The first manifestation is ingrained in contemporary culture. Sloth equals lazy. But if we understand sloth as the avoidance of the demands of love, we can understand the second manifestation of sloth—busyness. We can avoid mending our friendship by lazily not engaging, but we can also avoid mending our friendship by simply being too busy to make the time to think or engage the problem. Over-packed schedules and long to-do lists keep relationships at bay. We convince ourselves that we are productive people doing the right things. But when we are so productive that we no longer have time to carefully tend or foster love, we are developing a slothful character. Slothfulness, in this version, is manifested through avoidance.

So we see that by understanding diligence's roots of love, sloth is more than simply being lazy with to-do lists. Slothfulness rejects the demands of love through apathy or avoidance. But we must also be wary in how we define what we love. The virtue of diligence does not simply ask us to choose something we love and work at tending it. Diligence demands more of us—it demands that we attend to our *duty*.[3] In the Christian virtue of diligence, God has given humanity the duty to love God and love their neighbor as themselves.[4] Therefore, the Christian virtue of diligence does not simply let you foster your chosen love of video games while you make no effort to bring your neighbor, who you don't know very well, a meal when they are sick. Nor does the Christian virtue of diligence give a pass to a CEO, on account of her rigorous schedule, to not take an afternoon to knock on the door of her elderly neighbor and offer to keep her company. We are called to love God and love our neighbors. This takes effort. This is hard work. Any avoidance of this duty through laziness or busyness is the vice of sloth.

James was not lazy, but he was slothful. He was a hard worker, but so busy he could not, nor did he want to, afford the time to consider "love of neighbor" in his creative process. He placed the puzzle over people. He was slothful.

SLOTH AND EXPRESSIVE INDIVIDUALISM

James's business and attentiveness to his schoolwork brought him praise. Professors looked to him to set the standard, and students admired him for doing so. But as I got to know James better during his third year at the university, it became clear that he was not in it for the applause. He rarely smiled when classmates told him how good the project looked during peer critiques. He never visited my office seeking acknowledgment for his work. Frankly, I don't believe I ever heard James utter the words, "Do you like it?" James worked as if he had blinders on—unaware of the praise sent his way. James was driven.

James's drive served as a model to the fellow classmates who—at times—failed in their discipline, preferring social activities over school-work. Thus, when the administration decided to put a student panel together to speak to the incoming freshmen about ways to succeed in college, they asked James to join the panel first. He agreed.

James was joined by four other students on the panel, and myself, who acted as the moderator. The panel was to be held at 7 p.m., late by my standards, but still early in the evening for young students. As the clock moved toward 6:50, I surveyed the audience, finding no open chairs. Granted, the

3. DeYoung, *Glittering Vices*, 81.

4. Matt 22:36–40.

offer of extra credit certainly helped to drive up attendance. Nonetheless the freshman were there, hopefully open to hearing guidance from the student panel.

I, too, was glad to have the student panel that night. Serving as the moderator, I was given the opportunity to ask important questions to these students, and in the process get to know them better. The night would not disappoint in this manner. The student panel answered the questions with articulate enthusiasm—most of all James. It was this night that I learned what fueled James's drive.

To begin the panel discussion we started with basic introductions, followed by sharing humorous stories from their time at the university. We then moved to students describing what it is like to study their major. Midway through the night, one particular question spurred the panelists to reveal their deepest motivations. I asked, "Why do you guys approach school the way that you do?" James's answer was most revealing.

James started, "I work hard—as most of us do on the panel. We wouldn't be sitting here in front of you if we didn't. I guess my answer to this question is slightly boring. I don't have a super dramatic back story motivating me to change the world. I don't have a chip on my shoulder to prove to people I can do it."

He paused, collecting his thoughts. "Just like any of you, I suppose, I want to have a good and comfortable future. So, I looked at who I was, and what I was good at. I am good at creative strategic thinking. I can see the logic behind hard problems and find solutions. So, I figured this was my best bet in securing my future."

James shuffled in his seat. I sensed he was slightly uncomfortable in the spotlight. He continued, "So I decided to invest in myself. Really take the time and effort to develop myself. I figure between getting better at this, and my willingness to hustle, someone will pay me someday for it. Will I be rich? Who knows, but I wouldn't complain."

Bringing his thoughts to a close, he said, "How do I approach my studies? I invest in me as a means to invest in my future."

After James finished, the other panelists shared, as well. Following a few more questions, the night wrapped up with free cookies and casual conversation with the freshman cohort.

What motivated James to work harder, and hustle faster was an invested interest in his comfortable future. He did not care about the applause now, but hoped with anticipation for the economic applause in the future. And knowing James, I had no doubt this would come to fruition.

Slightly differently from other stories we have seen so far, James wasn't fully motivated by expressing his true self now. Rather, James was seeking to be true to his future self. This variant of being true to oneself is known as utilitarian individualism.[5] Utilitarian individualism understands a person's natural instincts for pleasure, comfort, and security as good. Thus, human life is about seeking to maximize the fulfillment of these instincts. To do this, efforts must primarily be put into advancing self-interests—with an eye toward economic ends. Life is fundamentally about self-development, and consequently, engagement with others is only considered useful if it pays future dividends.

As we have observed before, dedication to your perceived true self—whether now or in the future—can lead to vice within one's life. A life dedicated to the future true self is a life centered on fulfilling your inner desire for pleasure, comfort, and security through self-interested future economic gain. Yet as a result, there is little space left for the tending of dutiful love of God and neighbor, in the here and now. And because we prioritize future self-interest over our duty to love, habits of apathy and avoidance accumulate into a slothful character.

Here is where James struggled. For James, the puzzle over people mentally made sense to him because his ability to reach strategic and creative solutions was his path to his future self. Attending to the needs of his "neighbor" added extra variables to the creative solution—making it messier, less sharp. Or so he thought. As James began to learn in his last year of university, a creative process that does not lovingly consider other people is a disordered creative process. Such a process ultimately produces creative solutions that work in theory but not in practice.

SLOTH AND CREATIVITY

The process by which people develop novel, high-quality, and appropriately useful works is an arduous process. Creative solutions do not just appear, they are developed. Some ideas work, some do not. Many first attempts fail, only to reveal a new path forward. Unfortunately the faint of heart never stay with the process long enough to reach a level of completion. Creativity requires perseverance.

5. Bellah et al., *Habits of the Heart*, 32–33; 336.

After years of study, researchers have come to this same conclusion. Research results show that successful creatives share a very strong sense of perseverance when faced with overwhelming obstacles during the creative process.[6] Anchored in their sense of purpose, creatives work to complete the process and goals they have set for themselves.[7] This phenomenon is even observed in children who score high on creative scales. Such children are willing to dedicate longer and harder periods of work in order to accomplish their creative goals.[8] Perseverance, hard work, and commitment are key traits of creatives.[9]

James exemplified perseverance. He worked hard, fought through the creative obstacles, focused on the goals, redefined the problem when necessary, and developed creative solutions. Far and above his classmates who did not achieve this level of perseverance, James produced better creative solutions. Yet, to James's deep frustration, his final creative products consistently fell short. Reviewers and users appreciated the logic behind James's work, but time after time were quick to dismiss it as a fully viable solution.

After one such review, James stopped me on my way to my car.

He gently tapped my elbow to gain my attention and said, "Professor, do you know why this keeps happening to me? I work so hard, give everything to these projects. I don't stop until I resolve the problem. They are good projects, the reviewers say that."

Catching his breath from walking fast to catch me, he asked, "Why do they dismiss it so quickly? The solution works. Why doesn't it capture them like other projects?"

I responded, "James, we have talked often about what makes a successful creative work. At the most basic level, what are the three requirements for a creative work—by definition?"

Without hesitation, he answered, "A creative work is a novel, high-quality, appropriately useful solution."

"Good," I affirmed. "When the users or reviewers 'dismiss' your project, which of these three things do you think they are commenting on?"

Pausing to think for a minute, he responded in an unsure tone, ". . . appropriately useful?"

---

6. Csikszentmihalyi, *Creativity*.

7. Torrance, *Why Fly*, 141–52.

8. Winner, *Gifted Children*.

9. Gardner, "Creativity," 8–26.

"Right. James, you are very persistent in your creative process. And that is producing novel, high-quality solutions. But you are lacking in your diligence to others," I said.

James stopped in place, now under a large shade tree. I stopped with him, and asked, "How do you know that a creative work is appropriately useful?"

He quickly responded with confidence, "If it works. If the creative problem is solved."

"Maybe," I responded. "Something can work but not be appropriately useful for someone. An architect can design a high-end studio for an artist, only to discover the artist prefers to paint in the bathroom instead because of the quality of light. The studio space works, but it doesn't. Or another example, a musical score can be beautifully composed, drawing out deep emotions of sadness. But if the score is composed for a movie intending to depict the joy of friendship, the working score no longer works."

Pausing to ensure he was tracking, and sensing he needed more clarification, I offered one more example. "Let's say a scientist is faced with a perplexing puzzle on how to treat a children's disease. After much work, she discovers a cure. However, the cure requires injections every two hours. The solution works, but at the same time it doesn't work. A cure that requires constant injections for a child will have few adopters."

James nodded, tracking my point. He commented, "So to be a successful creative, I have to learn how to understand people to ensure that my creative solution is appropriately useful? Then I can be a successful designer."

"Yes, but no," I rebutted. "Yes, for your creativity to flourish, you must understand how the creative solution works for people. But no, you do not do this to simply become a more successful creative. If you approach the process of understanding others as a means to success, you will never fully understand others. By doing so, you are only concerned for others because it serves your interests. You cannot really understand someone if you don't actually care for them."

I paused to shift my bag from one shoulder to the other, relieving the growing soreness. I continued, "James, in order to really develop appropriately useful solutions, you must actually care about the other individual—desiring and seeking to know what it would be like in their shoes. Flourishing creativity requires empathetic diligence."

Over the next fifteen minutes, I switched my bag from shoulder to shoulder five times. As our conversation continued, James began to see that to create fully flourishing creative works, love of people must become the puzzle. If you approach the creative process as James did, the process is simply problem-solving. But to create flourishing works, "you must first decide not only what the problem is, but who has the problem."[10] And when you approach the creative process as an exercise in framing who has the problem, empathy becomes a key orientation.

Empathy, or the ability to understand and share other people's feelings, serves as an important part of flourishing creativity. Scholars studying the relationship between creative processes confirm that empathy plays a large role in creative achievement.[11] They have observed that by taking on another's perspective, the creative process is fueled by an intrinsic motivation which leads to highly creative ideas.[12] Or in other words, when we create for others, we are motivated not by selfish gains, but are driven to love and serve. Thus, by taking on another's perspective, we are more likely to develop ideas that are useful, as well as novel.[13] An empathetically driven creativity is a flourishing creativity.

The following semester, James still worked hard, but he worked differently. The development of innumerable iterations of the solution was interrupted by lengthy discussions with those who would engage the work at the end. James began to test his logic with others—learning that not everyone thinks the same. And he began to stop referring to the project solution as "my project," and began using phrases like "this project is for . . ." By the end of his fourth year, James had learned that creativity takes perseverance in the creative process and diligence in our duty to love. Perseverance and diligence fuel flourishing creativity.

EMPATHETIC DILIGENCE

Diligence to our duty to love God and love our neighbor is hard work. Apathy and avoidance come naturally to us. Laziness and busyness remove us from the demands of love. And the more we remove ourselves, the more our character is defined by the vice of sloth.

10. Adkins, "How Does Empathy Influence Creativity," lines 8–9.
11. Form and Kaernbach, "More Is Not Always Better," 54–65.
12. Grant et al., "Necessity of Others," 73–96.
13. Grant et al., "Necessity of Others," 73–96.

Moral vices can be understood as disordered loves.[14] In the case of many vices, a natural love of self, recognition, or security becomes magnified to an immoral level, producing vices such as pride, vainglory, and greed, respectively. But sloth is different. The vice of sloth is less of a disordered love than a denial of one's duty to love. The typical slothful action is an action that abandons love instead of demanding an immoral level of it. Sloth flees love.

Therefore, as we seek to uproot the vice of sloth in our lives, we must discipline ourselves to stay put, not flee. The spiritual disciplines employed to attend to sloth are habits that demand we stay in the midst of demanding situations, and habits that encourage us to see and care for others. The applied disciplines for sloth include the practices of *stabilitas loci*[15] and service.[16]

Stabilitas Loci

The vice of sloth urges us to escape from the demands of our duty. We prefer our own comfort over the hard work. We leave the studio or lab to head for a "break" at the coffee shop, thinking we will solve the issue at hand once we return after the break. We never return. When relationships get hard and we begin to fight with our significant other, we turn around and walk out of the room. Or in the case of the creative process, we present our creative solution to people who will engage with it. Once they begin to critique the work, we desire more than anything to simply leave—not hearing or learning how to serve them better.

The discipline of *stabilitas loci* is a Latin term for "stability of place." In this practice, the goal is to be attentive to your body, disciplining it to stay and not flee. By staying physically present we take the first step in training our souls to stay put and accept its duty. *Stabilitas loci* was a prescribed remedy for sloth in the monastic tradition.[17] In the monastic tradition, monks willingly submitted to the spiritual task of daily prayer and study. Monks sat for hours on end in their cells rigorously fulfilling their duty. But they were not superhuman. As the hours wore on their energy and enthusiasm for their duty waxed and waned. At low points, monks reported

14. DeYoung, *Glittering Vices*, 39.

15. DeYoung, *Glittering Vices*, 96–97.

16. Calhoun, *Spiritual Disciplines Handbook*, 144–47.

17. DeYoung, *Glittering Vices*, 97.

they were tempted by the idea of fleeing the monastery and returning to a life in the city. The demands of their religious life were hard. Sloth tempted them to physically flee their cell, and abandon their religious duty. To fight these temptations of sloth, monastic leaders called monks to the virtues of courageous endurance, long-suffering, and perseverance—starting by the simple act of physically staying put in their cells.[18]

Therefore, to attend to our slothful tendencies, we must discipline ourselves to have stability of physical place, thus training our whole selves to not flee.

Predetermined Time: Sloth flees when things get hard. To help fight this, we must not let our urge to flee rule. Intentionally set patterns of courageous endurance by predetermining the length of time you will dedicate to working on your creative process. Ensure that you set the time for a duration which you feel will be a challenge. If you typically flake out of a process after thirty minutes, set a predetermined time of one hour and fifteen minutes. If you typically work for an hour and a half, set a predetermined time for two hours. Even if things get difficult, or you have a desire to attend to other matters—stay put. Don't physically leave.

During this practice, there will be natural phases. First, it will seem easy. Then as the temptation to flee arises, minutes will seem like hours; the clock will not move. But if you persevere through, after a bit of time the clock resumes it normal speed. In many cases, if you courageously endure through the slow clock and reengage the process, the clock will speed faster than expected. Once the stability of place is mastered for a set time, increase the time.

Neutral Tuesday: Loving relationships present demands on us—demands we often push onto the other individual. Our natural inclination is to think that we are fulfilling our duty, while the other person is slothful in their efforts. To become more aware of how slothful we are in loving others, and to practice the art of *stabilitas loci*, establish a Neutral Tuesday. Invite the other person in your relationship to sit with you once a week. During this time, invite the other individual to freely share with you one item they really appreciate about the way you love, and one item where you could attend to your duty of love better. Offer to carry out the same exercise in return.

The key to Neutral Tuesday is to stay neutral. Do not get upset or aggravated. Listen well, and be open to identifying areas of sloth. It is

18. DeYoung, *Glittering Vices*, 97.

important that each of you only share one positive and one negative item. This is not a laundry list of aggravations. It is a time to focus on a particular area where habits can be changed—and character reformed. Perhaps most importantly, it is key that you physically stay put. Don't immediately leave the room after the exercise. Stay physically present for fifteen to twenty minutes with the individual after the completion. Practice stability of place—train yourself not to flee.

Service

Attending to the demands of love requires us to see others. Once we fully see, we can fully care. And once we care, we work diligently to tend to this love. Yet, as we have observed, slothfulness uses apathy and avoidance—shielding our eyes from fully seeing. To train ourselves in new habits, we must learn to see others through acts of service.

The discipline of service requires us to build the habit of "seeing" by acknowledging that the needs of our neighbors are as important as ours.[19] Through service we offer our "resource, time, treasure, influence and expertise for the care, protection, justice, and nurture of others."[20] And it is through these physical acts of service that we learn to see, empathize, and eventually love others. Acts of service fulfill our duty to love God and love our neighbors as ourselves.

For Me, for God, for Others: The process of character formation is partly a process of recognizing your patterns and habits. This exercise has two phases. In this exercise, divide a piece of paper into three columns, labeled "For Me," "For God," "For Others." Thinking over the previous week, write down any intentional actions that "served" someone in the proper column. Take note of the proportions between the columns. Keep in mind that "service" can be understood in small acts as well as large. Serving does not always mean volunteering at a food pantry each week, or traveling to a different country to provide humanitarian aid. Service can be simple acts of acknowledging that others' needs are as important as yours. This can look like taking an intentional ten minutes out of your busy day to talk with another individual that is downtrodden, offering to help another study for

19. DeYoung, *Glittering Vices*, 145.
20. Calhoun, *Spiritual Disciplines Handbook*, 144.

a class you are not enrolled in, or bringing food and coffee to a classmate unexpectedly. The goal of service is to sacrificially notice others.

In the second phase of the exercise, divide a new sheet of paper into the same three columns. Considering the next two weeks, write down acts of service in each column that you plan to carry out. Ensure that the "For Me" column has the least amount of entries. Be specific about who, and how, you plan to serve. After completion, reflect on the quality of the initial week versus the weeks of service.

Empathetic Service: Creativity is just as much about solving the problem as it is understanding whose problem it is. When faced with a creative problem, seek to identify the key constituency you feel is faced with the problem, or will most likely engage with the creative work. Prior to starting on the creative process, seek to gain empathy through engagement and service.

In order to move beyond simple observation and into a real understanding of their perspective, try to spend at least eight to ten hours with them. Join them during their day, both observing and mirroring them in their regular activities. During this time, identify a point where you could serve them in an impactful way. Take notice of particular ways that this individual is limited due to resources, skills, or access. See if you could serve in any of these areas of limitations. Can you use your creative talents to carry out a small project for them they cannot afford? Or can you complete a mundane task they do not have time to do? Can you introduce them to another professional with an expertise they need? The temptation during this exercise will be to consistently think about the creative project ahead. Resist this tendency and try to find an act of service that is not related to the project. Return within the next week to perform this act of service. Only once you have completed this shadowing experience, and performed an act of service, turn your mind to the creative process at hand.

In all the disciplines above, the intent is to stay and see; care and love. Building habits that allow you to accept the demands of love will shift your motivation and the focus of your creativity. Creative flourishing is defined by a diligent fulfilment of your duty to love.

• • •

Sloth is easy. Despite the fact that we all desire, and are capable of love, our natural inclination is apathy and avoidance. We fail in our duty.

But as James learned, correcting a slothful character doesn't simply mean working harder. Hustle will bring the creative process only so far. Creativity requires perseverance through the creative hardships, *and* diligence in the duty to love. When combined we can create novel, high-quality, and appropriately useful works. When perseverance and diligence are combined, our creativity flourishes.

5

Anger

CREATIVITY CATALYZES IMPROVEMENTS RANGING from life's small adjustments to large-scale world-changing ideas. For most people, creativity is primarily a personal process. In the course of our daily lives we encounter annoyances, problems, or inefficiencies. After enough encounters with the same issue, we instinctively begin to develop a creative solution. Most often this creative process goes unnoticed. When the rack in the dishwasher keeps falling down, we find a rubber band to tie it up. When our dinner table won't stop wobbling, we transform a cereal box into a table leg extension to stop the rocking. When we feel like our house feels a bit drab, we select a new paint color and matching decorations to liven it up. In most cases of everyday creativity, our creative process is personal.

However, when the creative process moves from everyday personal improvements into commissioned professional services for clients, the process cannot stay personal. No matter whether we are attempting to find a new chemical compound, design a building, create a brochure, or write a script for a promotional video, the production of a novel work must match expectations of quality and usefulness held by the "client."

Within the university setting, and within the course on creativity, students learn how to carry out creative processes for a client. But since students are just beginning to develop their creative skills, university courses typically do not have students offer professional creative services to a real external client. However, to simulate this, the professor, or a jury of experts, acts as a pseudo-client for the student. As students develop their creative works, it is regular practice that students present their work for critique or evaluation by the faculty. In doing so, students begin the critical transition from a personal creative process intended to improve their lives, to a transparent creative process intended to serve others; a transition that is often very difficult.

Most often, students that are entering into a university creative course have had successful experiences in previous creative endeavors. Up to this point, their creative works have been deeply affirmed by those around them—their high school art or STEM teacher, their admiring friends, and of course their family. In each case, these influential figures in the student's life tend to overly gloat about the greatness of the work, offering very little constructive criticism. So when a student in the creativity course presents their work to the faculty for an in-depth critique for the first time, the process comes as a bit of a shock. In response, students react in several stereotypical ways.

First, there is the weeper. This type of student will gleefully present their work, and with anticipation await the praise. But when the faculty begin to question, critique, and offer fundamentally different ways to see the creative process, their smile becomes flatlined. These students often become very quiet, putting every effort into keeping a stoic face—holding back their tears as long as possible. For some, within the first few sentences a small tear begins streaming down their face, while others are able to hold it in until they return to their desk. Once seated, in both cases, tissues are necessary to keep the table from getting wet. Rarely do these students have a large outburst; silent tears define the weeper.

Second, there is the confused student. This type of student has never really been forced to see the world outside of their own scope of vision. So when the faculty begin to invite the student to see differently, only unanswered questions remain. As the faculty ask leading questions, attempting to reveal a new way of seeing the problem, this type of student becomes confused. The student is only able to answer the faculty questions by repeating their original statements on the creative work. Then, when faculty attempt a more direct approach of overtly describing the revisions or alternative viewpoints, the student will again look back with a confused expression on their face. The student will ask clarifying question after clarifying question, trying to understand the faculty's comments. But no matter how many times the faculty rephrases the answers, the student is still left confused—unable to see their project in ways other than how they themselves see it.

Next, there is the excuse maker. This type of student inherently thinks that the creative process is like a simple math problem, with one correct answer. Thus, when the faculty begins to critique and offer new ways to see the problem, they feel as if they got the project "wrong." Although the faculty reinforce the idea that the presentation is not steadfastly wrong, but could become far more fitted in its usefulness, or elevated in its quality, the student misses the nuance. Thus, the student quickly responds with a laundry list of excuses as to why their offering doesn't exactly match the faculty's comments. Excuses, such as "I ran out of time," to "Yes, I was intending that but my computer file crashed," to, "That is what I meant to do, but . . ." Each excuse attempts to express that they were not wrong. Rather, it was other factors beyond their control that caused the project to not be perfect; it wasn't their fault.

Then, there are students who respond like Tess.

If you were to close your eyes and picture what a stereotypical creative person looked like—you would imagine Tess. Tess lived as if all of life was her creative canvas. It would be fair to describe Tess as brightly unique. Each time I saw Tess, her hair was a different color. Her sense of style did not conform to popular fashions, but was a conglomeration of things that caught her eye at the moment. Tess preferred to travel barefoot most of the time, feeling that footwear was an option despite convention or regulations.

Tess's overall personality matched her aesthetic choices—bright and expressive. Her sense of humor was intelligent, but quirky. She frequently contributed to conversations with easy laughter; feeling free from typical social convention. Tess smiled regularly, fully enjoying a life of creative expression. Overall, she was a joy to be around—except during critiques.

When it was time for Tess to present her work, she would head to the front of the class with a smile on her face. Proud of her work, Tess would provide a colorful, and adjective-filled, description of her creative solution. After which, she would often start to collect her work to head back to her desk, forgetting that the panel of faculty were there to critique her work. After a few steps with her bare feet, she would remember and return to the front. Once she was resettled, the faculty would begin their analysis, suggestions, and questions. They wouldn't get too far before Tess would interject.

With each point made by the faculty, she would launch a quick rebuttal defending her work. She would return questions with sharply pointed questions of her own. Her typically cheerful face would send nonverbal expressions of disbelief, annoyance, and disgust. Any faculty suggestions for how to improve the quality of the work would be rebuffed by a verbal reply as to why the suggestion wouldn't work.

During critiques, Tess would visibly morph from joy to agitation. As she became more agitated, the more closed she became to offers of constructive criticism. To anyone watching the scene, it was clear that with each passing minute, Tess was constructing walls between herself and the reviewers—seeking protection from perceived attack. And in doing so, she was shutting down her creative process by forgoing any sense of open-mindedness. Tess's creativity was suffering from the vice of *anger*.

THE VICE OF ANGER

Anger is such a common emotion, it may be hard to believe that it is on the list vices. But like all vices, when a natural instinct is practiced in a disordered way, vice develops in our lives. Anger is no exception.

Anger, in and of itself, is not bad. Even the Scripture's descriptions of God includes just anger.[1] When practiced righteously, anger is the fuel that fights injustice.[2] Motivated by love for others, anger is the proper response to recognizing that loved ones have been wronged. Recognizing this injustice, anger makes our hearts beat faster, sends blood to the face, and instills courage in us to set things right. Such passion stands up for goodness, truth, and beauty. Without anger, we often fail to engage our will in the fight for justice.[3] Proper anger drives forward rightful justice.

However, the strength of anger's passion can overtake proper discernment of its application—leading to a disordered expression and eventual vice. Anger can become disordered either through an excessive level of expression or in its application to the wrong thing. Or in other words, anger can become a vice if *how* we express it, and *why* we express it becomes disordered.

First, anger leads to vice when how we express it becomes characterized by the wrong amount; most often in excess. When we think of

1. John 2:13–22; Mark 3:1–6.
2. DeYoung, *Glittering Vices*, 118.
3. Aquinas, *ST* II-II q.158, a.8.

someone whose anger is out of control, we can easily imagine this disordering of anger. We picture a person red in the face, moving with exaggerated gestures, and yelling things they may not mean—taking out anything and anyone in their path. The aftermath of such excessive anger is only damage: holes in the wall, broken lamps, injured people, and scarred relationships. When anger boils over it blinds us from seeing rightly or acting with discernment.[4] Thus, when our anger is expressed in excess, our passion to seek justice and set things right ironically evolves into a new cause of injustice. Anyone that has been on the receiving side of such anger will quickly attest that this expression of anger is clearly a vice.

In addition to applying the wrong amount, the second way that anger becomes disordered is by applying it to the wrong target for the wrong reasons. Or in other words, the "why" of our anger can become disordered. If we understand righteous anger to be a passion for justice motivated by love for others, then unrighteous anger twists any real concerns for justice into the desire to simply serve the self. Such anger finds agitation at the slightest perception that someone is dishonoring us, or preventing us from our desires. When we feel that our honor or status is in question, our hearts beat fast and our palms sweat—preparing our bodies to protect us from attack. Yet, with such anger, we do not simply seek to ward off attacks through shielding, we ourselves attack back as a means of defense. We retaliate through counterattack, protecting our perceived selves and desires. We unleash the passion of anger on anyone that dares challenge us or interrupts how we think things should be.

After the dust settles, the vice of anger does not stop its bidding. Even though we are no longer literally swinging our fists, anger continues to blind us through the justification of our actions. We were right to get angry. We deserve what we were denied; we are owed due respect; such actions were needed to claim our rightful share.[5] Such justifications for the "why" of our anger are fundamentally expressions of self-promotion. When we give ourselves over to unrighteous anger the "why" of our anger becomes selfishness promoted as self-righteousness thinly wrapped in a pretense of justice. This self-focused and self-aggrandizing anger is a far cry from a passion for justice motivated by the love of others.

Righteous anger can very effectively drive a creative process. In such a case, anger is a controlled fuel driving the creator to develop the most

4. Cassian, *Institutes*, VIII.vi.
5. DeYoung, *Glittering Vices*, 123.

successful solution which may bring about goodness, truth, and beauty that is due to those they love. And in such a case, any critique is welcomed as an opportunity to reach this aim more effectively. Critique thus refines our ability to love well.

Yet for Tess, critique was not understood this way. The anger that welled up inside of her during critique was not an anger defined by a desire for justice motivated by love for others. Rather, her anger served as counterattack measures meant to protect her honor or status. The constructive criticism of the faculty was perceived by Tess as a dishonoring attack on her. She quickly built up a wall between herself and the critique. She closed herself off, preventing further creative development—effectively disordering her creativity.

ANGER AND EXPRESSIVE INDIVIDUALISM

Expressions of anger during critique are expected during the first weeks of the creativity course. Students are in transition from primarily serving themselves to learning how to serve others. So as the course progresses and students move further along in the process, there are far fewer instances of angry reactions. Unfortunately, this was not the case for Tess. She was as angry on day seventy-five as she was on day five—and by some accounts even more so.

As her anger seemed to accumulate over the weeks, I became concerned—fearing the potential of an unconstructive public outburst during class. The following week would prove my fears correct. Tess's anger did overflow. However, my prediction of an outburst during class was incorrect. The outburst came, of all times, while I was finishing lunch in the cafeteria.

There I sat alone, finishing a sandwich at a table for four. Just three minutes prior, two other faculty were sitting at the table with me. But as the clock approached 1 p.m., they left to head to their afternoon classes—leaving me to finish my last few bites. With one small bite of sandwich left in my hand, a flurry of colorful clothes and purple hair swooped into the chair across from me. Unaware of the conversation about to rapidly come at me, I placed the last bite of food in my mouth—rendering me unable to speak.

Tess stared at me, clearly agitated. As I chewed, she began, "I just don't get it! Every time I put my work on the wall, the faculty launch critique after critique at it. No matter what I say, the work is bad or wrong or could move in a different direction."

I sat there listening; chewing faster—hoping to speak and deescalate the conversation.

Despite her denial of normal social protocol, fortunately, Tess wasn't a yeller. She continued with an appropriate volume, but still aggressive tone, "My family loves what I do, my friends love what I do. I even send my work to my old art teacher, and she says she likes it, too. Why is it different here?"

Swallowing, I asked, "Tess, does your work develop and change from the first day you start to work on it to the time when you are finished?"

"Yes, of course," she responded.

"So do you think that any work is perfect during the creative process?" I inquired.

She replied, "No, it changes. It gets better as I work on it."

"Tess, this is what critique is all about. It is a part of the creative improvement process. In any creative process we need to be looking to advice from people who are experts in the field, or clients, who are the experts in how the final solution will work," I said.

Having calmed down a bit from her initial level of agitation, she said, "I put in a lot of effort to improve my work. I just don't understand why the faculty doesn't like me. Every time I put up my work it feels like they tear it apart."

As she was speaking, I was wiping my mouth. I replayed her comments to myself in my head, unsure if I had misheard her. I asked, "Could you say that again, I may have missed what you said."

Clearly irritated, she said with slight exaggeration, "Why don't the faculty like me? They always tear apart my work during critique."

Unfortunately, I had heard correctly. Tess had just asked why the faculty didn't like *her*. I quickly responded, "Tess, our critique on your work has nothing to do with whether we like you or not. We are providing constructive criticism of the work—not you as a person!"

My comments did not immediately compute. She stared back at me, as if I had spoken a foreign language.

When Tess asked why we didn't like her as a person when we critiqued her creative work, she was conflating two very different things—herself and her work. But as a person who sought to "be true to herself" in every aspect of life, to Tess, her work was herself. Tess's objection was revealing a primary assumption of expressive individualism.

As we have explored in previous chapters, expressive individualism calls an individual to place their inner desires and passions as the source of right and good. Furthermore, once an individual has bracketed out any external influence, the act of "being true to yourself" requires action. This is the "expressive" part of expressive individualism. With the self as the source, one's identity is constructed through the expression of inner passions and preferences. By successfully expressing yourself, you become your authentic self.

Thus, when Tess asked why we didn't like her as a person because we were critiquing her creative expression, she was operating from an expressive individualist set of presuppositions. When Tess produced her work, she was producing herself. So any critique on the work was a full frontal attack on who she was; and anger ensued. She felt justified in her anger because she felt the comments confronted her very authenticity and self-worth. Tess held to the underlying idea that the purpose of her creativity was to define herself.

By holding these sets of presuppositions, Tess was vulnerable to the vice of anger. The anger she was expressing was a self-focused anger intent on defending who she was. Living with an expressive individualist mindset, Tess was unable to experience righteous anger within the creative process. Her anger was not motivated by love for others, and thus could not drive her creativity forward by accepting critique. Instead, her anger built up walls of defense, closing herself from critique. And by closing herself off, she was unable to live out a fundamental attribute needed for flourishing creativity: open-mindedness.

ANGER AND CREATIVITY

Innovation and novelty require a creator who can see beyond the known reality and perceived limitations. It takes an individual who is open to new ideas to imagine that steam could be utilized to propel a cart with wheels forward. Such creators see the world as they know it while simultaneously remaining open to imaginative ways in which something can become incrementally better. Whether through challenging commonly held presuppositions or combining known things with disassociated ideas, creative individuals are open to new possibilities. Such possibilities, in the hands of an open-minded creative, quickly transform our daily lives from the task of drying food, to using a block of ice to store food, to relying on electric-powered refrigerators to preserve food, to now providing the ability for refrigerators to examine their own contents and communicate any food needs with an owner via the internet. Without the attribute of open-mindedness, novelty could not be achieved.

Beyond casual observation, research scientists have rigorously documented the relationship between open-mindedness and creativity over the past fifty years. Scholars have observed that successful creative individuals are characterized by their openness to experience.[6] Such open-minded people flexibly engage with ideas around them, observing and utilizing combinations of stimuli that others ignore.[7] Or in other words, open-minded people are more curious and motivated to explore the world, finding new possibilities in the process.[8] These observations have led scholars to conclude that open-mindedness acts as a prerequisite for creativity.[9]

With this observation, though, it is important to understand that an open-minded person is not simply a sponge that takes in anything it comes into contact with. Open-mindedness does not require a person to hold truth as relative, foolishly accept any idea, or forfeit the courageous stewarding of a successful idea through a gauntlet of detractors.[10] Instead, a virtuous open-mindedness is able and willing to temporarily suspend their own perspective in order to give a fair and impartial consideration of an alternative viewpoint.[11] By allowing for an honest hearing of a different viewpoint, a person is able to properly discern the appropriateness of adopting, integrating, or discarding the viewpoint. Thus, at its core, open-mindedness freely admits that we could be wrong, elevating the pursuit of goodness, truth, or beauty above self-pride.

Virtuous open-mindedness, as with all virtues, requires both willingness and ability. Commonly, people desire and have a general willingness to be open-minded—recognizing the benefits to life and creativity. However, when faced with an alternative or competing idea, most find it difficult to actually suspend their own perspective in order to give an honest hearing to the alternative. There are many sources preventing us from our ability to be open-minded, one of which, as described above, is pride. Additionally, within the context of creative development, another major factor that

6. Kaufman et al., "Openness to Experience," 248–58; Silvia et al., "Assessing Creativity," 68–85.

7. Peterson et al., "Openness and Extraversion," 1137–47.

8. DeYoung, "Openness/Intellect," 369–99.

9. Rokeach, "In Pursuit of the Creative Process," 66–88.

10. Baehr, "Open-Mindedness," 30–52.

11. Baehr, "Structure of Open-Mindedness," 191–94.

prevents our ability to live out open-mindedness is the anger that arises when our work is called into question. When anger boils over, it blinds, "the eyes of our heart," preventing us from seeing the good in alternatives, seeing our own faults, and seeing righteousness.[12]

After my lunchtime conversation with Tess, her demeanor seemed to soften a bit during class. I do not know if she fully understood how she was conflating critique of her work with a perceived critique of who she was, but I hoped she would begin to see the difference. To help her in this process, when the next project came along, we decided to slightly modify the assignment for Tess.

Midway through the semester in the creativity course, we pair students up and ask them to carry out a creative process within their discipline focused on developing a solution that serves their partner. The intention is to have students practice offering creative services for an external client, and in doing so, practice the art of empathy. However, knowing Tess's struggle with critique, we felt this project may also serve to re-form how she understood creative critique.

Normally, each student is paired with a student they do not know well. This allows for greater opportunity to practice empathetic methods. However, for Tess we modified this standard—pairing her with her best friend. It was our hope that by carrying out a creative process motivated to serve someone she loved, Tess may successfully separate her perception of her creative work from her identity, and be open to hearing ideas that may improve her ability to serve her friend. Fortunately, our hope was fulfilled—but not without some bumps along the way.

Midway through the project development, students are asked to present their project for faculty critique. Again, we modified this for Tess. Instead of just the faculty formally offering constructive criticism, we invited her friend to also sit on the panel. Watching Tess during this critique was like watching a person wrestle with multiple personalities.

After her presentation, as usual, the faculty began to offer ways in which the creative product could improve in its quality and approach. And, as normal, Tess's smile morphed into a thin line of agitation. Her anger was blinding her from hearing these alternative ideas. She was constructing walls between her work and critique. Before the walls got too high, we invited her friend to offer some constructive criticism on the project. As the

12. Cassian, *Institutes*, VIII.vi.

friend offered alternative ideas, often aligned with the faculty suggestions, the walls melted between Tess and the reviewers. Her scowl softened, and her body language changed. She was listening, and actually being open-minded—discovering new ways of seeing the project which could better serve her friend.

As the review continued, Tess oscillated between anger and open-mindedness. When the faculty spoke, Tess's instinct was to bristle. When her friend spoke, her instinct was to love. Fortunately, as the review carried on, the openness to love ultimately prevailed.

After the review, I approached Tess, asking, "Tess I appreciate the way you handled the review today. Did it feel different to you?"

She quickly said, "Yes, it did. I liked having my friend on the review."

"Why do you think that made a difference?" I inquired.

She paused for a minute thinking. She then said, "With her critique I didn't feel attacked. I really want my final product to be good for her. So when she made a suggestion I felt it was important to listen."

"That's a good observation, Tess." I continued, "Why does it feel different when the faculty provide critique? Just like you, we want your final product to be the best it can be for your friend. So we are offering suggestions of how to improve your work, drawing from our years of carrying out creative processes. We hope that you can learn from mistakes we have made in the past. We want your creative work to be good for your friend—and any other client you eventually serve."

"I never thought of it that way. It just always felt like I was wrong, and the faculty were telling me I didn't meet their standard. It felt like I wasn't good enough," she explained.

"Tess, we are all pursuing goodness, truth, and beauty with our creativity. We want you to do well in this pursuit. We want you to be able to love well through your creativity. I think today's critique was different for you because you were motivated by love. And because of this, the most important thing was to make the project good for your friend. No matter whose idea it was, you were open to considering it because you wanted to love your friend well. This is what critique is all about," I offered.

She nodded along, offering one final word prior to heading to her next class, "It was nice not being so agitated during the critique—it was actually a fun process to think through other ideas." And with that she left with a smile.

The modified critique provided Tess an experience of just how open-mindedness fuels creativity. Granted, there was no magic conversion moment for her—or any of us. Pursuit of virtue is a long process, and fleeing from vices does not happen in fifteen minutes. At times during the course, Tess still got agitated and angry. But she started to learn that it was important to not allow anger to close her off. And in those moments that she was not blinded by the vice of anger, Tess's open-mindedness began to foster a flourishing creativity.

GENTLE OPEN-MINDEDNESS

The vice of anger blinds us, closes us off, and forcefully pushes others away. As we seek to guard ourselves from the overflow of such unrighteous anger, we must attend to each one of these effects. The process of pruning the vice of anger is a process whereby we learn to restrain and resist.

In contemporary culture, there is a commonly held idea that anger is a passion that must be expressed for fear that it will overflow. We call this "venting"; evoking the mental picture of steam pressure being released from a system. Interesting though, the Christian tradition of pruning moral vices offers different advice on the matter. Within this tradition, the act of "venting" is not thought of as a healthy practice, but a moral mistake. Anger, like other passion-based vices, becomes ever more present in our lives the more we indulge it.[13] The more we "vent" the more we practice the passion, making it easier next time around. With enough practice, a.k.a. venting, it eventually becomes nearly impossible to actually restrain what has grown into an unruly part of our character.

Therefore, the process of pruning the vice of anger from our lives includes spiritual disciplines which open our eyes to the truth of our actions, and invite open-minded interactions with those around us. By accurately recognizing where anger is present in our lives, we become aware of what to resist. Further, by inviting open-minded interactions we deny the desire to "vent," replacing such actions with a virtuous counteraction. The applied disciplines for anger include the practices of *self-examination* and *confession*.[14]

---

13. Aquinas, *ST* II-II q.142 a.2, as described in DeYoung, *Glittering Vices*, 121.

14. Calhoun, *Spiritual Disciplines Handbook*, 91–94.

Self-Examination

The first step in learning to resist an unwieldy passion that blinds us is to become fully aware of its presence in our lives. The discipline of self-examination is a process whereby we become open to God's revealing of our true nature.[15] Self-examination is not a "neurotic shame-inducing inventory."[16] Rather, it is an intentional grace-filled time of observation where we seek to recognize how and why a vice manifests. In the privacy of a relationship with a forgiving God, we are able to drop the facade of self-righteousness, and perform an honest evaluation of our condition. Self-examination leads to self-awareness, which enables us to self-restrain.

Anger Journal: In order to recognize just how much unrighteous anger is present in our lives we must intentionally observe our anger. In this exercise, dedicate a small journal to the private exercise of observing anger.[17] Over the course of three to five days, notice when anger manifests in the regular course of life. Manifestations can be overt outbursts, times where you "vent" to your friends, or even simple feelings of agitations that arise. With each manifestation briefly record (1) the intensity of your anger from one to ten; (2) the situation in which the anger arose; (3) why you were angry; (4) why you feel justified in your anger. Don't labor over, or wordsmith, the notations. The goal is to capture the passionate essence of the manifestation. Be honest; no one will ever read this journal.

After carrying out this exercise for the predetermined set of time, put the journal out of view for a period of a week. Resist the temptation to return to the journal until a full seven days have passed. Once the week has passed, set aside some time to review the journal. Review the entries—now with some distance and a cooler head. Notice any patterns or trends. Observe the primary way anger is manifested in your life. Evaluate whether your anger is fighting for selfish reasons or is seeking justice for those that you love. Honestly determine what percentage of your anger is selfish. Write down any observations in the pages that follow. Set aside the journal—returning to it, and this exercise, periodically throughout the following months.

15. Calhoun, *Spiritual Disciplines Handbook*, 91.

16. Calhoun, *Spiritual Disciplines Handbook*, 91.

17. DeYoung, *Glittering Vices*, 133–34, discusses the practice of journaling anger, and shares the author's experience with the practice.

Open-Minded Barrier Identification: Within the normal course of a creative process, numerous ideas are tabled for consideration, with some being utilized and others cast aside. This exercise aims to intentionally evaluate whether your creative process is being fueled by open-mindedness, or is fundamentally closed to any external ideas. To do so, dedicate every other page within your creative journal to self-reflection. Over the course of a normative creative process, carefully document the key ideas that are considered for the development of the creative work. With each idea, notate where the idea originated from—categorizing each idea as either self-derived or externally provided. Following, under each idea provide one to two sentences of rationale for acceptance or denial. Be as reflective and granular as possible for this one project. Don't attempt to belabor the explanations; simply capture the essence at the time of the decision.

Following the completion of the creative process, return to the journal. In one sitting, review the notated process of idea acceptance or rejection. Look for any patterns or trends. Observe how open the process was to external ideas. Evaluate whether you were able and willing to suspend your perspective to give the ideas an honest hearing. Following the review, take one page in the notebook to record any observations from the exercise, recognizing your level of open-mindedness.

Confession

The process of self-examination is a process of recognizing the presence of vice in our lives. Following this recognition, the discipline of confession is a process of publicly admitting our complacency to the vice, and intentionally working toward change. The Christian tradition we have been exploring advocates that confession is good for the soul. Yet, that doesn't mean it is easy.[18] We have a vested interest in appearing to be morally good to those around us. Confession radically removes this façade, exposing our wrongdoings. However, if we are brave enough to practice this spiritual exercise, we loosen the grip of vice on our lives.

Seeking Reconciliation: Manifestations of unrighteous anger cause destruction. This exercise seeks reconciliation in the wake of our anger through confession to those that we have harmed. Utilizing the anger journal created in the self-examination exercises, identify one instance of selfishly

18. Calhoun, *Spiritual Disciplines Handbook*, 91.

motivated anger in your recent past. This manifestation does not have to be a large outburst, or have caused undue property damage. The manifestation can be as small as feelings of unrighteous agitation that were never expressed. Identify an individual to whom your anger was directed. After obtaining their agreement to talk, confess to them that your anger was driven by selfish aims. Make no excuses or justifications. Acknowledge that the anger effected them, and apologize. Let them know that you are actively seeking to prune the vice of anger from your life, and that you appreciate their forgiveness.

Depending on the level of original destruction, there may be a variety of reactions to the confession. Certainly a difficult reconciliation process may ensue if the damage was great. But even if the individual is indifferent on account they did not even know you were angry, don't dismiss the gravity of the vice. Confession is the recognition of the severity of vice. After courageously completing your first act of confession, seek to establish the exercise as a regular practice in your life.

Seeking Open-Mindedness: In a fashion similar to seeking reconciliation, seeking open-mindedness looks to rectify our error in being closed-minded. Referencing the design journal completed in the open-minded barrier identification exercise, select one particular instance where you dishonestly dismissed an external idea without giving it due consideration. Identify the individual who provided the idea, and ask if they would be willing to discuss it further. At the start of your meeting, practice the discipline of confession. Acknowledge that you were previously closed-minded about their idea, without any further justification. Apologize for your disposition, and ask for their forgiveness. Following, invite them to share their idea again, this time promising that you will be more open-minded about the idea.

When the individual is presenting their idea, clearly indicate you are attempting to understand: take notes, ask questions, and reiterate their idea to ensure that you understand correctly. Following the meeting, attempt to understand their idea further by hypothetically applying it to your previous design. By exploring what affect the idea would have on the creative work, you will fully engage with an open mind. Even if you still decide the idea is worth dismissing, reflect on the process of confessing and being open-minded. Be aware of future instances of closed-mindedness, and attempt to follow these instances with additional acts of confession.

The intent of the disciplines above is to recognize, reconcile, and restrain unrighteous anger in our lives. If we fail to do so, we run the risk of being blinded by its affects—ultimately disordering our creativity. By intentionally fostering open-mindedness in the place of unrighteous anger, we are able to foster creativity that flourishes.

• • •

Anger has the potential to either fuel our creativity or close it off from flourishing. When we put ourselves at the center of it all, anger serves only to destroy any barriers to self-service. Yet, if love for God and our neighbor is our foundational motivation, anger is very effective in bringing justice, and spurring our creativity.

Tess experienced both poles of anger. When she viewed creative critique through a self-focused lens, unrighteous anger ensued—closing her off from creative development. When love for her friend became the motivation, however, her creativity flourished through her willingness to fully consider any idea that could help her love better. Through these opposing experiences, Tess ultimately discovered that restraining unrighteous anger allows virtuous open-mindedness to contribute to the development of a flourishing creativity.

6

Lust of the Eyes

IN THE BROAD VIEW, the university is an exciting place. It is a place where inventions are made, new knowledge discovered, and truth pursued. On any given day, from any corner of the university, a world-changing theory or practice can emerge. Eager students join passionate professors, and together a palpable excitement is formed as they pursue truth.

However, the day-to-day work required to generate these break-throughs is far from exciting. Most days are filled with long periods of solitary quiet reading and writing; professors alone in their offices; students quietly working in their study carrels, studios, or laboratories. Yet, the work is far from sleepy. The anticipation of discovering truth holds real stimulation; a slow-burning anticipation. In general, on an average day at the university, most people's heads are down, focused on their work.

Late summer a few years back, on a particular nondescript Monday, I played my role in this drama—head down, focused on developing a new set of lectures for my students. Two hours had passed since I started my deep focus when I sensed some oncoming eye strain. I stopped my work, and stood up to take my customary walk to the window to let my eyes fall to the distant horizon. But on this day, where I normally saw green lawns and people casually walking by, I saw a group of people forming into a semicircle on the sidewalk, pointing at one of the university lawns.

Eager to see what the commotion was all about, I headed out of my office to join the growing crowd. A few minutes later when I arrived at the scene, the crowd was thicker—rendering it difficult to see past. Fortunately

I was able to shuffle myself near the front, and look between the two heads in front of me.

There, lying in the grass approximately twelve feet from the sidewalk, was a half-eaten corpse of a rabbit. Regally standing atop the dead creature was a very large red-tailed hawk. As the crowd stared, this hawk unapologetically dissected the rabbit with his sharp curved beak, eating fur and all.

Unlike the inquiry happening in the surrounding academic offices, the crowd was not there to find new truths about the natural world. No one was taking notes, or carefully observing the effectiveness of the hawk's curved beak. No one was appreciating majesty of God's creation. We were gawkers of the mangled corpse, easily thrilled by the spectacle.

Strangely attracted to the event, the crowd stayed in full force for at least ten minutes—eyes peeled; staring. When the rabbit was reduced down to just few tufts of fur, both the hawk and the crowd started to leave. The crowd was tightly packed together, having jockeyed for a good viewing angle. So now, as people tried to leave there was a good bit of accidental bumping. As I turned to head to my office, a female student in front of me whipped around to walk the other direction, attempting to squeeze through a small parting in the crowd. Her turtle-shell-like backpack protruding from her shoulders was unfortunately not as petite as her. As she slipped passed me without as much as word, the backpack sent its greetings with heavy thump into my stomach. She paused, and turned to apologize. It was Anna, one of the students from my upcoming creativity course.

"I am so sorry, I didn't mean to hit you, Professor," Anna said apologetically.

Having recovered from the blow, I noticed the blunt instrument that hit me. It was a good-sized backpack, the kind one would wear on a longer hiking trip. The bag was made of black fabric, but very little of the fabric was visible. Sewn all over the extent of the bag where patches of flags, cities, and landmarks. I commented, "Wow, Anna, that's quite a collection of location badges."

"Thank you! Every time I travel to a new place, I collect a badge to show I've conquered it. This bag is kind of my trophy case. See here is the Europe section, Asia starts somewhere over hear, and American landscapes are all over," Anna proudly showcased.

"Impressive," I said.

Anna continued, "I love these experiences. My life's motto: 'The more you see, the more you be.' Wasn't that hawk devouring the rabbit amazing?

I have great photographs. I can't wait to show my friends. I even got a great self-photo of me with the bird in the background. I am National Geographic. Ha." She laughed.

Starting to head to her next class she turned her head to say the final farewell. "Goodbye, Professor, I'll see you later this week for class. I'm looking forward to being creative." With her bubbly smile, she turned and left.

As I headed back to my office, I was glad that Anna would be joining my class on creativity. Successful creative individuals are known for their curiosity and openness to new experiences. By the looks of her backpack, Anna was a very curious individual with much exposure to new experiences. She should fare well in the course, I thought, as I reached my office door.

But as I learned that semester, and so did Anna, curiosity can be a very positive driver or a false preoccupation within the creative process. Individuals whose curiosity is motivated by learning from experiences are able to successfully transfer ideas into their creativity. Anna could not.

Anna's curiosity suffered from the vice: *lust of the eyes.*

THE VICE: LUST OF THE EYES

The phrasing "lust of the eyes" is at the same time familiar and unfamiliar. Lust may be a familiar concept, but "of the eyes" is most likely a new set of terms. Prior to examining how this vice affected Anna's creativity, let's take some time to fully understand this vice.

Contemporary culture is well acquainted with the general notion of lust. In its most common conception, lust is associated with sexual desire. Contrary to the Christian conception, which holds lust as a vice, contemporary culture frequently utilizes lust as an economic virtue—marketing products via lust, selling periodicals and movies with lustful narratives, and using lust as a tool of celebrity self-promotion. Sensual lust is an ever-present part of society. This is the concept of lust we are familiar with: giving your body or mind over to illicit cravings or desires, particularity sensual in nature.[1]

Yet, lust of the eyes is different in that it seeks, and gives, into a different set of desires.[2] Sexual lust is of the flesh, finding pleasure in ways only

1. Cook, *Seven*, 15.

2. 1 John 2:16 details three primary ways that humans are tempted by vice: lust of the flesh, lust of the eyes, and pride for life.

possible through bodily senses.[3] Lust of the eyes, on the other hand, is a *desire to see, or know*. Lust of the eyes is "a kind of empty longing . . . which aims at not taking pleasure in the flesh, but at acquiring experience through the flesh."[4] This lust does not seek sensual pleasures, but the pleasure of finding out and knowing.

Whether sensual desire, as in lust of the flesh, or lust of the eyes, these desires are generally found in all of humanity. But, as the concept of vice identifies, these natural desires can become unbalanced, excessive, and ultimately immoral. In the case of lust of the eyes, the desire to see or know becomes disordered either through the content of what we seek, or our motivation for seeking.

First, our desire to see or know can easily become tempted to seek out content that is not good, true, or beautiful. What is a naturally good desire gets twisted by a lustful longing to see "what is not in the ordinary sense pleasurable at all."[5] As the common saying goes, this type of curiosity kills the cat.

Flickers of this disordered curiosity show up almost daily in our lives. We are tempted to give in to lust of the eyes when we overhear whispers of gossip as we walk down the corridor. Temptation springs a desire in us to stop and "know" more about what was said—leading to full participation in destructive gossip. We are tempted to give into lust of the eyes when we hear of someone performing mystical signs and wonders, and desire to go see. We deviously desire to know when we wonder how humans would respond to designed experiments of suffering, or what it would feel like to commit a crime or take illegal drugs. And, in a final example, we fall to the lust of the eyes when we cannot peel our eyes away from horror.

I was guilty of this when I joined the crowd around the hawk in the university lawn. We were gawking at the site of an hawk devouring a rabbit not to admire its goodness or beauty. Nor were we there to recognize God's amazing creation. The crowd regularly responded to the tearing of the rabbit's flesh through audible cries of "Oh man" and "Poor rabbit." Our disordered desire to see and know was not interested in the pleasure of recognizing truth. We were drawn to the horror of the mangled corpse.

This attraction to horror plays out every day in our lives. Granted, we don't run to see mangled corpses every day of the week. But we do turn our

---

3. Meilaender, *Theory and Practice of Virtue*, 134.

4. Augustine, *Confessions*, 10.35.

5. Meilaender, *Theory and Practice of Virtue*, 135.

attention to news media that runs scenes of horror in a continuous loop. Or we watch horrific accidents compiled in video clips for entertainment. On the weekends, we pay large sums of money to watch films that intentionally manipulate our emotions, allowing us to know how it feels to be in horrible life situations. Arguably, in average contemporary culture, our desire to know and see is more frequently fulfilled in a disordered way than not.

No matter the ultimate source of devious satisfaction, our natural desire to see and know can fall to lust of the eyes easily—diverting us from seeking goodness, truth, and beauty.

Second, or desire to see or know can become lustful due to the disordering of our motivations. In this case, it is not the content that becomes disordered, but the drive behind our curiosity that becomes twisted. The virtuous motivation of this natural desire is to seek understanding or acknowledge God. A properly ordered desire to know focuses on the pursuit of truth through acts of learning. However, lust of the eyes distorts these motivations into simply desiring to possess the experience of knowing. Or in other words, we seek out experiences not in order to understand truth or acknowledge God's goodness more fully. Rather, we seek out experiences simply for the thrill of seeing. We greedily long for new kinds of experiences.[6]

Because this is a motivational manifestation of lust of the eyes, even when pursuing good content, our pursuits can be disordered. We can be curious about what it would be like to be in a different country, and thus arrange travel to visit. With a virtuous motivation, we travel in order to learn about the other culture, understand their way of life, observe God's diversity of creation, and reflect on any understandings that can be applied to our life or home situation. Conversely, we could also take this same trip with disordered motivation to see and know. In this case, we travel in order to take pictures to show others, say we have been to such a location, or have a story to tell upon return. This motivation can be described as an "empty desire to possess."[7]

In another variation of disordered motivations, we may "seek to know something of benefit to many others; yet we may be moved not by thought of their benefit but by our desire to see."[8] To conduct a scientific experiment to learn how nanotechnology could be used in dense liquid may potentially

---

6. Meilaender, *Theory and Practice of Virtue*, 139.

7. Augustine, *Confessions*, 10.35.

8. Meilaender, *Theory and Practice of Virtue*, 139.

serve as a key understanding in future medicine. However, if the researcher carries out his curiosity with the motivation to simply see if it's possible, without motivation of others' benefit, he may be seeking an empty desire to possess knowledge. Or in a more mundane example, we could seek to learn elementary sign language. This can be done from a motivation for communicating and building community with the hearing impaired. But with disordered lustful motivation, we learn to sign for selfish reasons such as resume building or impressing others. With this motivation, we only learn a few phrases—which is enough to impress. Our curiosity is thin. This is unlike curiosity that has a virtuous motivation fueled by our care for others, driving us to continue learning and understanding.

Lust of the eyes distorts our natural desire to see and know by tempting us to seek the illicit, or skewing our motivations such that we simply desire to possess an experience.

LUST OF THE EYES AND EXPRESSIVE INDIVIDUALISM

As the summer gave way to the fall semester, the course on creativity started back up—this semester with Anna sitting in the second row, flashing her bubbly smile to all around. Typically students enrolled in the course come from a variety of majors spanning the extent of the university. While the diversity is good, it does mean that students generally don't know each other at the start. For a class that hopes to foster creative collaboration, strangers sitting next to each other is not ideal. So, within the first few weeks of class, the students are given assignments to introduce themselves in a memorable and impactful way—with the hopes of moving classmates from strangers to collaborators.

Each year, students introduce themselves in amazingly creative ways. Students in the past have written and produced full music videos, painted life-sized works, presented short stories, and invented a new material substance whose characteristics matched their personality. And, as this semester offered students the same opportunity, similarly creative approaches to self-introductions emerged. Anna's self-introduction was no exception.

When it was Anna's turn, I called her to the front of the class. She jumped up, exclaimed, "Give me one second," and bounced out of the room with a fit of energy. When she returned all you could see of her was a large grin and pair of bright eyes. Anna had gone into the hallway to don a costume that she had made for her introduction. The costume stretched over head and down past her knees. Rendered slightly immobile by the extent of the costume, Anna could not bounce to the front per usual. Instead she shuffled her feet rapidly back and forth, propelling her to the front. When she reached the front, she turned to show the class her costume. Anna had transformed into a life-sized version of her backpack.

"Hi, my name is Anna," she said cheerfully. "I live life by the motto 'the more you see, the more you be.'"

A smile was brought to my face remembering her energy the day this very same backpack was pummeled into my stomach.

She continued, "So the best way to get to know me is for me to introduce my backpack that I use every day. There is nothing particularity spectacular about the backpack itself. It is a normal pack you can buy at any store. But what is important is what is on my backpack."

Slowing a bit to catch her breathe from the excitement of speaking in front of class, she continued, "On my backpack, as you can see, are all of these patches. Each patch represents a different place that I have seen and experienced with my own eyes. I have been to common places and uncommon places."

Over the next five minutes, she continued to describe a couple of her favorite places, detailing what there was to see, and whether she liked it or not. Concluding her presentation she said, "So see what makes me unique, what makes me, me—just look at these collection of experiences. What I see is what I be—and I have the photos to prove it."

With her typical sparkling smile and animated movements she returned the larger-than-life backpack to the hall and took her seat, pleased with her presentation. I too was pleased with her presentation. It was creatively impactful. And now, I wasn't the only one with vivid memories of this famous backpack.

As the initial impact of the presentation settled, and as classmates moved into asking questions of her, a crack in her life motto was revealed. Anna's difficulty with some questions began to show that her life motto of "the more you see the more you be" wasn't a slogan for a virtuous desire to see and know, but was a by-product of expressive individualism.

After introductions, students are allotted free time to go and talk with someone that presented that day—to get to know them better. During this time, a number of students gathered around Anna, desiring to hear more of her exotic tales. She happily shared and answered question. Interestingly, though, Anna didn't fully track with all the questions. She had no problem answering questions such as, "What did it feel like to . . ." or "What was your favorite thing you saw when . . ." But questions like, "What is your biggest lesson from . . ." and "What differences did you learn to appreciate when you saw . . ." were difficult for her. Her typical answer to these later questions, as I listened in on the conversation, was something like, "I don't know, all I know is what I saw and liked . . ." or "I don't know, I just wanted to have the experience of . . ."

Over the course of ten minutes of casual conversation, it became clear that Anna's curiosity was thin. The patches on her backpack did not represent her desire to seek understanding or acknowledgment of God's creation. Rather, the patches represented her desire to own a large set of experiences by which she could be uniquely define herself by. Anna had an empty desire to possess.

As we have explored before, expressive individualism finds the path of an authentic life through the expression of one's uniqueness stemming from innate desires. In Anna's case, she was following her heart to see and know; a good and innate desire we all have. But the demands of expressive individualism modified this desire to become lust of the eyes.

Virtuous motivations to see and know drive an individual's curiosity to focus on understanding the creation and acknowledging the Creator. In this motivation, curiosity works to inform your recognition of the good, true, and beautiful which are inherent in the object or experience. This observation of external sources of right and good then acts as a reinforcement of the one standard found in God.

Yet, this stands in stark contrast to the motivations emerging from expressive individualism. Expressive individualism denies any external standard of right and good. The only authentic thing one can do is feed instinctual desires. Thus, a person's desire to see and know is not about observing external right and good, but is an expression of the self which must be lived out for its own sake. Therefore, what we seek to see and know becomes mere collection of experiences that act as a by-product of our desires; defining our uniqueness. And thus our curiosity falls to the lust of the eyes as we seek an empty collection of experiences.

Anna's patches on her backpack did not represent a curiosity which led to understanding. Anna's patches represented a desire to collect and possess experiences which could define her. And, as Anna discovered in the following weeks of the class, the practice of consuming empty experiences does not enable the creative process to flourish. Lust of the eyes empties creativity of its generative power.

LUST OF THE EYES AND CREATIVITY

As the weeks progressed in the creativity class, Anna's enthusiastic spirit proved to be an uplifting force for the class. She arrived with a smile and left with a new friend each session. Her enthusiasm for life was contagious to all around.

I was particularly thankful for her attitude when we arrived at the point in the class where I assign a relatively unpopular task. Granted, it is not the type of task that people rebel or speak out against. But it's the type of assignment that feels "in the way" to young, eager creatives. It is the task of studying precedent examples of the intended creative output.

Precedent studies come near the start of the project, right when enthusiasm is high. Typically when we discover a creative problem or task, we find initial excitement in the possibilities of solutions. Our minds begin racing, developing initial sparks of ideas. We lose sleep on account of our inability to shut down our internal creative brainstorming. Some even liken it to the same feelings of a new love relationship.

But, as most creatives have learned through experience, our creative process will fizzle if we simply rely on the high. Again, it is similar to the process of a new relationship. If a relationship is to last and grow in depth, we must transition our initial shallow giddiness into deeper emotions of care and concern. And this process is partially fueled by developing a virtuously motivated curiosity.

As many scholars have noted, curiosity is potent because of its fecundity—or ability to trigger other actions or sentiment.[9] It is interesting to note that the Latin root for curiosity is *cūrāre* meaning "to take care of," and is shared by other-regarding activities such as "care" and "cure."[10] When a person overcomes indifference, and fosters a curiosity that reverently desires to understand, it leads people to a new level of caring—effectively fueling a flourishing creative process.

That is the intent. Precedent studies help students transition from initial project excitement into effective curiosity. But for students who are not used to this transition, it feels like the initial rush of new love is being

9. Baumgarten, "Curiosity as a Moral Virtue," 171.

10. Baumgarten, "Curiosity as a Moral Virtue," 171.

torn from their life. Students' desire to stay in the place of initial infatuation leads them to grumble over the need to analyze previous work. Fortunately Anna was in the class.

For this assignment, we often ask students to go and experience a precedent in person—whether it be a painting, work of architecture, commercial product, or performance. When hearing this, Anna immediately started darting her head back and forth, holding small whispered conversations with the students sitting next to her. Before I was even done explaining the assignment, she had coordinated several excursions with different groups of students. Although I would have preferred if she had done this after I finished explaining the assignment, I was slightly pleased that at least a third of the class was not looking at me with annoyed expressions.

The following week, students were asked to share what they had learned from their experience and study. As students walked in, Anna passed by me at the front of the class. She stopped and pointed to her backpack saying, "Look, Professor, a new patch—from our precedent excursion. It was fun!"

As class started, I asked if anyone would like to go first. Anna's group volunteered. They proceeded to give a very colorful account of their time—including tales of misadventure when they got lost in the heart of the city. Each student took the time to share their feelings of the precedent, "I liked it . . . ," "It wasn't my favorite . . . ," and so forth. The focus was firmly on their experience and personal reaction to the precedent—which is good and important, but not the only intent of a precedent study.

Hoping to steer the conversation into new territory, I asked the group, "So what did you learn from studying the precedent? Can you give one example of an aspect of the creative work that was good, or beautifully fitting for its context? What is one key understanding that you are taking from the experience that could be applied to your creative considerations?"

Now, to be fair, having worked with many early creative students, I wasn't expecting a robust answer. Most early students have not yet developed an ability to be effectively curious. And frankly, my questions for this first group served primarily as a warning call to all following groups to develop these ideas quickly prior to presenting. Yet the lack of ability to answer these questions served as a predictive measure of the creative process to follow.

Anna, like many of her classmates, appreciated the experience of the seeing the precedent, but quickly forgot the intent as they moved onto their creative process. Once reunited with self-ideation, the projects moved along, albeit slowly. Once a student manifested their original spark of an idea, there was little motivation or developmental possibility remaining. For these students, when the high of creative process falls and the infatuation ends, there is no curiosity to fuel the creative process.

The precedent study example above serves to illustrate the broader relationship between curiosity and creativity. As we noted previously, curiosity has the ability to fuel other actions—including creativity.[11] When our curiosity is motivated by a "reverent desire to understand creation,"[12] we uncover insightful understandings of the right and good which can be used as fuel for our creative process. By virtuously fulfilling our desire to seek and know, we learn from the unfamiliar and the discoveries enliven us, deepen our care, provide us with applicable principles, and drive our creativity.

However, this fruitful relationship between curiosity and creativity can turn sour. A lust-of-the-eyes-affected curiosity leads to a disordered creativity. As we saw in previous examples, a curiosity motivated by a "longing to possess the experience of knowing" shortcuts the process of curiosity. If the motivation behind our curiosity is merely a "greedy longing for a new kind of experience," or motivated simply by "enjoying the act of seeing itself," we fail to gain insight or understanding.[13] We are easily satisfied. We only desire possession. Thus, the process of curiosity either stops on account of achieving enough to showcase, or stops because we have reached an experience of knowing—albeit a shallow one. In either case, we stop being curious, stop being inquisitive, stop seeking further understanding.

And without a regular flow of insights derived from curiosity, our creative process falters—relying solely on the limited frame we already possess. If we operate from a curiosity defined by lust of the eyes, our creativity dries up, starves for fuel, and ceases to flourish.

PURE CURIOSITY

Although we may have never heard the term "lust of the eyes" before, it is one of the most prevalent temptations in our current culture. Not a day passes when we aren't faced with the invitation to see and explore knowing illicit things. And because of this, we have become so desensitized that we

11. Hardy et al., "Outside the Box," 230–37.

12. Meilaender, *Theory and Practice of Virtue*, 140.

13. Meilaender, *Theory and Practice of Virtue*, 139, 143.

fail to recognize illicit as illicit—except for the edges of the extreme. And soon after these edges become normalized, and we become curious about further-off edges. Ironically, a virtuous person would be beyond grateful that they avoided seeing or knowing some of life's worst offerings. But today we eagerly shell out money and dedicate our time to experience them. And with these repeated acts, seemingly innocent wonderings build and shape us until one day our curiosity is so disordered we are unable to satisfy our curiosity with the good, true, and beautiful.

And if the illicit doesn't fully disorder our curiosity, the temptation to simply possess the experience will. Satisfied with the mere enjoyment of seeing, we fail to fully recognize the depth of God's offerings in creation. Once we succumb to either of these temptations, our curiosity is ruled by the lust of the eyes.

Lust of the eyes is like a disordered appetite—similar to our dinner appetites. We all feel hungry around dinner time, and this is natural. To fulfill this hunger we have two options. First, we can feed it a healthy nutritious meal with the proper understanding that food is not just about what happens in the mouth, but what it does for our bodies. At the end of this meal, we feel full, satisfied, and well-functioning. Or second, we could feed our appetite with junk food, sweets, and empty calories simply because it initially tastes good. However, as we all have experienced, despite eating more than we should, we are not full. Our appetite remains. So we feed it more junk. The process continues until we feel sick.

Now if we continue feeding ourselves junk for long enough, when we actually discipline ourselves to eat a healthy meal, we still feel a bit unsatisfied. We still long for the junk. But, as anyone that has ever attempted a diet can attest, your perception of food changes quickly. At the beginning of the diet, a carrot is tasteless. But after ceasing to consume artificially sugary food for a while, the carrot tastes sweet and satisfying. After a few weeks of healthy eating, junk food that you once craved so much loses its appeal. Healthy food is once again satisfying. But it takes time and discipline to reorder your appetite.

A disordered appetite to see and know works in a somewhat similar fashion. Curiosity shaped by lust of the eyes habitually fulfills its desire to see and know with empty or illicit calories. And because of this, we feed it more and more. And despite our increased levels of curiosity, we never feel satisfied and eventually make ourselves ill. Just like our hunger appetites, change requires that we avoid junk and readjust our understanding of the purpose of food. And just like a food diet, it takes discipline and time to reorder your curiosity.

Once we recognize the presence of this vice in our lives, the act of pruning lust of the eyes requires that we stop feeding our curiosity with empty calories, and start retraining our curiosity to seek goodness, truth, and beauty. To do this, the spiritual disciplines employed restrain empty calories from our curiosity and work to retrain our curiosity to recognize— and eventually crave—virtuous understanding. The applied disciplines for lust of the eyes includes *fasting*[14] and *celebration*.[15]

Fasting

The discipline of fasting intentionally designates a period of time during which you deny yourself something. The process of fasting is an intentional act of denial, but perhaps more so, is a process "that reveals the thing that controls us."[16] Through denial we resensitize ourselves and begin to rediscover the satisfaction in purity. For our present case, we begin to recognize the disorder of our curiosity, and begin to experience the value of pure curiosity.

Illicit Media Blackout: A disordered curiosity regularly gives in to the temptation to see and know something that is not good, true, or beautiful. Yet, as with most disordered appetites, we do not notice just how far we have traveled down the path. To begin to recognize how far we have come, this discipline intentionally stops seeking to fulfill our curiosity with illicit material. Set aside a predetermined set of time to be focused on fleeing the illicit. Because we are unaware of our desensitization, seek to completely shut out, or turn away from, any possible fulfillment of disordered curiosity. Turn off media, avoid movies with illicit themes, change music that glorifies violence, do not play video games you would feel uncomfortable playing with a four-year-old, and don't participate in laughing at videos that compile peoples' accidents. Quickly you may notice that your entertainment options become very limited.

As with any fast, it is recommended that you start small at first. Challenge yourself to successfully fast for one day to start. After reflecting on

---

14. Calhoun, *Spiritual Disciplines Handbook*, 218–22.

15. Calhoun, *Spiritual Disciplines Handbook*, 26–28.

16. Foster, *Freedom of Simplicity*, 174.

your experience, attempt a two- to three-day stretch. Become aware of just how much you crave the junk. After a series of progressively longer fasts, take notice of your changing appetite to see and know illicit things.

Stop the Search Engine: As we have seen, a lust-of-the-eyes-driven curiosity desires to have the joy of simply knowing—not fully understanding. In contemporary culture this approach to curiosity is practiced regularly, and reinforced through quick satisfaction of answering any curiosities via an internet search. This fasting exercise seeks to deny yourself this quick satisfaction by intentionally not turning to the internet for answers. When a question arises in your mind, or you begin to wonder about something, do not turn to the internet for an answer. Instead, carry around a notebook. When you begin to wonder, write the question down on its own page. Stop and think about the question for a while. Write any secondary questions below the first. Jot down any thoughts you may have on the topic below, as well. Attempt to keep the fast for five days.

By not quickly satisfying your curiosity, you will be tempted in two ways. First, you will be tempted to break your fast and search online. This is the expected temptation, so you should be mentally prepared to resist the urge. The second temptation is less overt, but just as dangerous. By not immediately satisfying your wondering, you will be tempted to simply forget about it. Don't let this happen—don't give up on your question because you couldn't possess the enjoyment of knowing. Return to the question on a daily basis. Add more thoughts and questions below the initial question. Look for connections between the pages of notes. Develop new questions that connect several pages together. I trust you will find that by the end of the five days, you have a much more interesting set of questions to explore online than your original wondering. You will begin to experience pure curiosity.

Celebration

Lust of the eyes builds patterns in our lives where we give our attention to, and lift up, things that are not good, true, or beautiful. We do not relish in the experience nor enjoy the goodness of the creation and its Creator. Similar to other vices, lust of the eyes shapes our lives through habits of misplaced worship. Or in other words, a life shaped by lust of the eyes celebrates the wrong things in the wrong way.

The discipline of celebration seeks to intentionally celebrate the right things in the right way. The discipline of celebration seeks to take "joyful and passionate pleasure" in the radically glorious nature of God and his creation.[17] Through intentional celebration of the good, true, and beautiful we grow our capacity to recognize, enjoy, and serve God—particularly through our curiosity and creativity.

Celebration Notes: In a life shaped by lust of the eyes, we habitually avoid goodness by seeking the illicit or thinly possessing experience. We need to retrain ourselves to see things differently and care differently. This exercise has two parts—one wide in scope, the other deep. The first part seeks to train you to recognize differently. In a notebook, challenge yourself to observe and write down fifty instances of the good, true, or beautiful you encounter in your day. Attempt to identify these instances throughout the course of the day, and not just in one sitting. Have the notebook handy, ready to jot down an observation right after it occurs. After completing this during the normal course of your day, seek to vary your day. Let your feet wander and your mind wonder what is around a different corner. Take different paths, visit different places, talk to different people—and when doing so, observe instances of the good, true, and beautiful. Attempt to do this for five days straight.

In the second part of the exercise, at the end of each day, review the recorded observations. Choose one that particularly stood out to you. Take out a loose sheet of paper, and write a note to the person, place, or event. Describe in detail what you observed, and how it exemplified goodness, truth, or beauty. Make sure you identify at least three reasons why—celebrating the instance with descriptive adjectives. Avoid writing what you felt about it or how it made you feel. Simply celebrate the goodness, truth, or beauty. If it is about a person or event, attempt to deliver the note to a person involved.

Truth, Goodness, Beauty Party: The discipline of celebration seeks to teach us to increase our enjoyment when we lift up the right and good. And in doing so, it starts to adjust our habits of being satisfied in possession of knowledge, moving us toward a desire to delight in understanding goodness. While this can be done in a solitary, reflective manner, celebration is often most effective in community. To practice celebration, in this discipline seek to identify something good or right. Attempt to identify something

17. Calhoun, *Spiritual Disciplines Handbook*, 11.

99

that may go unnoticed or is not usually communally celebrated. Once you have identified this, plan and throw a big party to celebrate it. Invite a large group of people over in its honor. Give toasts to its goodness. Have people go around the room to share words of admiration about it. Play joyful music. Relish in its truth, goodness, or beauty. Acknowledge it as a gift from God.

The object of celebration can vary widely. It can be a celebration of the beauty of a particular place or creative work. It can be a celebration of a mundane job well done. It can be honoring someone for an act of appropriate honesty. It can be a time to share and lift up kind words others have spoken. No matter the object, the point is to experience deep joy for truth, goodness, or beauty in such a way that you learn that understanding and recognizing the right and good is more satisfying that simply possessing.

• • •

Our natural appetite to wonder and seek, if virtuously formed, can lead us to a higher level of understanding, care, enjoyment, worship of God, and creativity. Virtuous curiosity is a wonderful driver of much good in life. Unfortunately the temptations found within a lust of the eyes can easily disorder our curiosity by tempting us to seek the illicit, or skewing our motivations such that we simply desire to possess an experience.

And when this happens, as Anna experienced, no matter how much zest you have for life, if you habitually practice disordered curiosity, creativity stalls. Only when we practice pure curiosity can our creativity flourish.

7

Greed

CREATIVE PROCESSES ARE OFTEN thought of as a means to an end; the way that creative individuals come by a novel, high-quality, and appropriately useful final product. And while a good creative process does effectively produce successful creative works, creating a photo-worthy final product is not the aim of the creativity course. The primary goal of the course on creativity is to teach students to think differently; to see creative potential in areas they had not noticed; to formulate ideas fluently.

With this aim in mind, at the start of each class session, students are exposed to a variety of idea-generation exercises. These exercises ask students to practice their divergent thinking in order to stretch their explorative creativity. For example, students are asked to imagine a standard object, like a bowling ball. Students are asked to write down as many different ways a bowling ball can be used. A timer clock projected on the wall pressures the exercise, and calls all students to stop after a few minutes. Once complete, the students share their ideas with the class.

In other exercises, students work toward becoming more fluent in combinatorial creativity. To do so, students are provided two very distinct, and sometimes opposing, things. Then again, with the timer clock lording over them, they must quickly develop a creative mash-up of these two things. Or in a similar exercise, students practice combinatorial creativity in real time by generating a series of phrases as a class. In this exercise, one student starts by sharing a phrase. Following, any student can add a phrase to the first. After the first two students, the following student must somehow combine the previous two phrases to generate a hybrid. The process repeats until everyone in the class has contributed, and we find ourselves in very different conceptual territory than when we started.

Or, a personal favorite of mine, these beginning exercises teach students to identify hidden assumptions as a means to increase fluency in idea generation. These types of exercises come in a wide variety of entertaining options. On some days, students are provided a riddle and asked to work on it until they see the hidden assumption that unlocks the riddle. Or on other days, students are asked to write down an observation, identify an assumption underlying the observation, and then work to craft a joke playing off of the identified assumption. On joke day, the intended short exercise gladly becomes an extended period of laughter.

While these exercises are fun, they do take a lot of concentration. Learning to think differently is not something that can be done while multitasking. Thus, prior to these exercises, we ask students to complete their own ritual to mark the transition between life and learning. There are few things more entertaining than standing at the front of the class and looking out as students carry out their unique pre-rituals.

In one corner of the room, one student yawns with mouth wide open, attempting to fully wake up. In the other corner of the room a student indiscriminately sweeps everything off their desk, throwing it all quickly on the ground. A few rows forward, a student wearing workout clothes performs some arm stretches to prepare. And all throughout the room, students desperately check their devices for any last communications from their friends prior to hesitantly putting them away.

Then there were students like Liam. Liam sat in the second-to-front row, always appearing alert and attentive. He did not yawn, stretch, or check his device—but he did have a distinct pre-creative exercise routine which matched his general demeanor. If Liam were to be described in two words, it would be "put together." Unlike the majority of his classmates who often rolled out of bed minutes before coming to class, Liam was always well groomed, sporting wrinkle-free clothes and up-to-date fashions. His care for aesthetic details, mixed with a naturally charming smile, could easily qualify him for a career in modeling. Liam was the picture of refinement—and he had a routine to match.

Each day prior the creative exercises, Liam would carefully set his environment. To start, he would take his hand and sweep the desk in front of him, ensuring its cleanliness. Next, he would reach down into his bag and grab four items. Prior to lifting the items to the desk, he would fulfill a small mental checklist for his backpack; zippers closed, standing fully upright, leaned against the leg of the chair, no straps in the aisle. Observing Liam, one could almost hear him mentally say, "check," as he went through each step. Following, he would bring the four items to the desk—one pencil, one pen, one eraser, one notebook. Each time, Liam would put them in the same locations—notebook open to a blank page, centered; pencil one inch from the notebook, pointing to the rear of the class; pen one inch from the pencil, pointing to the front of the class; eraser above the notebook, perpendicular to the notebook. After these were set, he would touch each item again to ensure they were straight, and then look toward the front of the class, ready.

And ready he was. Liam would consistently generate more ideas than the average student. When it was time to share ideas, he was often the first—and fourth—and seventh—to share. I was quite surprised when Liam appeared to be one of the quietest students when time came to share initial ideas for their first major project.

In order for students to become more cognizant of their creative process, during the course of a project, students are asked to share ideas and progress within small groups. Through the act of describing the creative process, students begin to learn the subtleties and mechanisms of creative development. These group discussions are planned at several points of the project, including initial idea generation. So when time came for the initial group sharing, I split the class into small groups to share.

Ten minutes into the exercise, students started becoming comfortable, and the volume in the room rose as ideas were bounced back and forth in the groups. Wanting to hear some specific ideas being discussed, I took to walking between groups to listen. On my first round, I noticed that Liam was quiet—but didn't think anything of it. On my second circuit around the room, I verbally encouraged Liam to participate. On the third walk around, I was pleased to see Liam begin to generate ideas with his group—although without much passion. On the fourth pass through, I found out why.

When I walked over to Liam's group, I happened to stop to listen, positioned behind Liam. From this vantage, I could see Liam's notebook on his lap in front of him. In the natural course of looking around, larger text at the top of the page drew my attention to his notebook. On the left page the header read, "Ideas to share." Under this heading there were a few generic ideas. On the right page the header read, "Good ideas for myself." Under this heading was a longer, more varied list.

As I listened to his group, Liam was participating. However, his participation lacked the enthusiasm he put into the opening exercises. All of his comments were tentative, dispassionate, and very generic. As I looked closer, it appeared that all of his comments he was sharing were being drawn from the left-hand side of the book. Never once did I hear him share ideas from the right side. Liam had intentionally separated his idea generation into good ideas for himself and uninspired ideas to share with others. Even when it was his turn to describe his ideas, he again chose a throwaway idea to present to the group for further development. Liam was hoarding the best ideas for his project, unwilling to offer up what he felt where the best ideas for group development. In his unwillingness to share, Liam was seeking to ensure a tidy creative process characterized by sole ownership of what he felt were the best ideas. Although Liam's quest for an orderly process were fulfilled by his tactics, as the following weeks would prove out, the desire for sole ownership of an idea would really limit his creativity from flourishing.

Liam was suffering from the vice of *greed*.

THE VICE OF GREED

When we think of the vice of greed, images of an old miserly man counting coins comes to mind. Or perhaps, if we were asked to point out greed in the contemporary world, we would point to someone who decides to buy a third luxury car and doesn't think twice when she rolls past a homeless person on the way home. Although if we were a bit more honest with how we thought of greed, we would also think of our "need" to have a walk-in closet in our bedrooms to store all of our clothes.

In all of these cases, greed is primarily identified by the excessive accumulation of things—whether it be money, cars, clothes, or anything else money can purchase. While this is not in error, the act of excessive accumulation is a mere symptom of a deeper disordering. Like all vices, greed is a matter of the heart, and our actions are simply a manifestation of such character.[1] Thus, when we fail to tip our waiter an honorable amount, we are not simply motivated by the desire to keep more money in our wallets. Rather, we are motivated by a disordered desire to ensure our free ability to

1. DeYoung, *Glittering Vices*, 101.

purchase snacks at the movie theater to follow. Similarly, when we spend hours figuring how to put more money away for retirement without giving a single thought to the huge numbers of children dying from starvation, we are not just motivated by counting coins. In such a case, we are motivated by a disordered desire to rely on ourselves to secure our future. Greed, accordingly, is the disordered and excessive desire for freedom and security.

Freedom is an alluring ideal. No one wants to be denied their ability to fulfill their desires, and thus people go to great lengths to ensure such freedom. Most commonly in the case of greed, people attempt to ensure their freedom through the excessive accumulation of wealth, or other items that money can buy or influence, including credentials, social positions, and self-promotion. The vice of greed persuades an individual that if they are able to accumulate and want for nothing, they would then be truly free to do as they wish. Yet, as the wisdom of the ages teaches, this is a half-truth.

Yes, with enough money, there is a certain amount of freedom to be had. However, this is not true freedom; possessions have a treacherous tendency to flip the script. As we accumulate more, we cease to own our possessions, but instead our possessions come to possess us. An increasing amount of things require an increasing amount of attention, upkeep, additional finances. And when the vice of greed seeps in, an increase of things only serves to grow our appetite for more until it possesses our thoughts and desires and distorts our perception of needs.

The opposing virtue to the vice of greed is generosity—or liberality. It is interesting to note that the Latin root of the term "liberality" is the same for our term "liberty" or freedom.[2] Thus, as the language indicates, there is a correlation between generosity and true freedom. Generosity, or liberality, is true freedom in the sense that a person is fully free from the grip of desiring more, and the vice of attachment to excess. And in such freedom, we are able to fully and effectively live out our purpose as humans to love God and love our neighbors. It is only through the pruning of the vice of greed that the desire for freedom can be achieved.

In addition to freedom, greed is a disordered desire for self-ensured security. Similar to freedom, the vice of greed tempts an individual to believe that their ultimate welfare and fulfillment of their needs is solely dependent on oneself. In this individualistic view, trusting in community, or in God's provisions, is not sufficient; one must rely solely on the self. Thus, the vice of greed convinces us to trade our trust in an all-powerful

---

2. DeYoung, *Glittering Vices*, 101.

Creator for trust in our human capabilities. Slowly, as we begin to shift our trust from community and God to the self, our contentedness in God's provisions erodes until we are left with a do-it-yourself approach to happiness and security.[3] Yet, in doing so, we limit ourselves from receiving God's blessing and full intent for our lives. Only by trusting in something other than ourselves and our possessions can we achieve a flourishing life.

Although greed most often manifests in its excessive desire for money as a means to freedom and security, greed can manifest in other ways, as well. As Liam demonstrated with his divided notebook, it is not only money that can provide the false promise of security and freedom. For Liam, sole ownership and possession of "good ideas" seemingly gave him a way to obtain his own security and freedom.

Specifically, Liam's act of hoarding ideas was an act of self-reliance. By not sharing his ideas for group development, Liam was attempting to secure the future of his project from two potentialities. First, Liam desired sole ownership of the idea was a means to protect from the possibility that someone else would present a project with a similar idea. Second, Liam was unwilling to share his ideas for group development in order to ensure his vision for the project remained intact. In both cases, he greedily put a tight grip on his ideas to ensure his ownership remained; he trusted himself only and not his community.

Additionally, when Liam divided his ideas, offering only the ones he didn't care about for group development, he was manifesting an excessive desire to secure his freedom. When an idea is offered up for group development, rarely does it come back the same. More often than not, the idea that returns is not beautiful or tidy. Questions are asked, alternative visions cast, and approaches are morphed, providing key potentialities for further development; the process is messy. For the put-together Liam, this was simply too messy. In such a process, the original creator offers to the group some control of the direction of the idea, sacrificing some authorial freedom in return for expanded creative idea generation. But Liam was unwilling to sacrifice his control over how the project progressed. In the eyes of Liam, such a sacrifice was simply too much. In order to ensure his total freedom, Liam greedily hid his ideas from the light of the group.

The vice of greed is fundamentally bait and switch. Greed promises security, but provides it only through diminished horizons. Greed promises freedom but ultimately ensnares. And unfortunately for Liam, he fell

3. DeYoung, *Glittering Vices*, 101–2.

completely for the bait and switch. Greed lured Liam by promising "security" of his ideas and the "freedom" to develop them into what he thought would be the best creative solution. Yet in reality greed limited Liam's creative development, denying him the creative flourishing.

GREED AND EXPRESSIVE INDIVIDUALISM

Seeing Liam's greedy notebook was alarming, but it didn't worry me too deeply, knowing that students tend to hold tightly onto ownership of ideas at the early stages of their creative skill development. Furthermore, the second part of the creativity course is designed to counteract this impulse through a group project. Dreaded by all students of all ages, the group project forces students to share and collaborate on ideas. Granted, this is the ideal version of the group project. But even in practicality, when one student attempts to take over and do most of the work, the leader is still forced to implement other ideas from the group, if even in a trivial way. Knowing this was the next part of the course, I simultaneously smiled and empathized with the challenge Liam was about to face, especially after seeing his notebook.

The group project assignment reveal occurs the same day as the final presentations for the first individual project. Excitement and pride is palpable in the room as each student shows off their final creative work. But as soon as the words "group project" are spoken, it is as if someone knocks the wind out of the room. Smiles turn to nervous glances around the room as students immediately begin strategizing about with whom they should partner if given the chance. I expect this type of reaction; collaboration is hard.

With the announcement, Liam mirrored his classmates' worry, but was amplified in his nervousness. Normally stoic and refined in his expressions, Liam gave into his impulses and dropped his forehead into his hands. With the sudden movement, his pencil was knocked out of alignment. He didn't even move to nudge it back into place. There was a level of distress in Liam that I was not used to seeing. So when Liam rushed to the lectern after class, I was not surprised.

"Can we talk, Professor?" Liam asked with an anxious tone.

"Yes, Liam. Let's go take a walk." I offered, hoping the movement and fresh air would help to calm his nerves.

I led Liam outside into one of the smaller and more private university courtyard lawns. Finding a weatherworn bench under a shade tree, I initiated the conversation as we started to sit.

"Liam, I get the sense that the group project is worrying you. I know that you are aware of this, but when you leave the university nearly all creative projects are group projects. Learning how to collaborate, work together, share ideas, and codevelop solutions are important skills. I know group projects are challenging, but I trust you will learn during the process," I said attempting to set the tone for the conversation.

As Liam ran his hands down the thigh of his pants to smooth out a wrinkle, he said, "I can't agree with you more, Professor."

To be honest, I did not expect his response. Out of pure curiosity, I replied, "So what seems to be troubling you? You seem anxious about the project."

"I know that I am particular in how I like things done. I know that it bothers me when things are not as they are supposed to be. And this is something I must continue to work on. Group work helps me with that. Even though it is hard for me, I know it is a good medicine," Liam reflected.

I was impressed by this young man's self-awareness and willingness to learn. But I was still unsure what was giving Liam trouble. Just as I was about to ask, he continued, "You are right, Professor, I am worried. I know that group work is the majority of post-college employment, and I have to learn how to do it well. But the reality is that I have to get a job before I can be in a group. And to get a job, I must have a really good portfolio. If I spend a lot of time on group work, then I lose those weeks where I could be making another project for my portfolio. I just feel like group work will hold me back."

Seeking clarification, I asked, "Do you feel like the group work will not be high enough quality or up to the standards of a portfolio piece?"

"Not really. Some of the projects can turn out well. The problem is that group work does not represent who I am, so I can't really include it," Liam lamented.

"Unpack that a bit more for me, Liam," I requested.

"The work I produce is my unique style, my approach, my voice. If a company wants to hire me, they should see my work so they know who I am. Group work muddles things by mixing my voice with others. It diminishes my portfolio. So while I know group work is a key skill, I need to spend my time on developing myself and my voice. Group work distracts from this," Liam explained.

Liam was breathing easier now that he had vocalized his thoughts. After smoothing the wrinkle in his pants one more time, he said, "My portfolio must show who I am, and to do this, I must own the project, do my process, and produce in my voice."

As the conversation wrapped up, I thanked Liam for sharing his thoughts with me. He pleaded one final time to not be required to do the group work. When I shook my head no, he thanked me for listening and again expressed that this is a key skill he needs to work on. With that, Liam was off to fully join the messy process of group collaboration.

While Liam's personality made him naturally uncomfortable with the messiness of group work, it was a much different set of worries that drove him to approach me that day. Liam was concerned that group work would mute his voice, which would not allow potential employers to know who he was. Liam desired that his portfolio be "true to himself," so to speak. And in doing so, he was living out the tenants of expressive individualism.

As previously discussed, expressive individualism conflates a person with their creative work. This line of thinking purports that a person's authentic identity is revealed when a person expresses their unique voice. No external set of duties or expectations contribute to one's identity. A person's authenticity comes from expressions of individuality.

So when Liam was worried that group work would muddle his authentic self, he was professing the philosophy of expressive individualism. The result of Liam's desire to be solely focused on developing his own voice led him to create the right side of his notebook. Liam believed that he must have complete ownership of his creative process in order to be authentic. And the only way to ensure this was to hoard the good ideas, hiding them from group development.

Liam actively denied collaboration and clung on tightly to ownership of his creativity and perceived authenticity. With each passing project, his grip tightened, and the vice of greed grew in his life. The demands of authenticity put forth by expressive individualism naturally led to the vice of greed in his approach to creative ideas, creative process, and eventual creative products. And as a result, Liam's greed prevented him from successful collaboration and a flourishing creativity.

GREED AND CREATIVITY

The ability to generate divergent ideas is a key skill for creative development. Through practice and training, we are able to become more capable of generating a higher number of quality and creatively novel ideas. For example, when tasked with developing alternative ways of using a bowling ball, someone skilled at ideation can develop a wide array of different ways to view the object in a short period of time. Such skills in divergent thinking fuel creativity.

Through regularly exercising our ideation muscles, our divergent thinking improves in four ways.[4] First, we become more fluent in ideation. Or in other words we are able to generate an increasing number of meaningful and relevant ideas. When we try to identify different ways to use a bowling ball our overall list grows from ten to thirty ideas.

Second, we grow in our flexibility. In such a case, we do not just see the bowling ball as a ball. Rather, we are able to see different characteristics of the bowling ball as new categories for ideation. For example, once we exhaust new ways that a bowling ball can act like a different kind of ball, strong ideation skills would then move to another category. For example, we could move from the category "ball" to the category of "heavy." In doing so, we unlock a whole new set of ideas: bowling ball as a door stop, paperweight or a can crusher.

Third, as we grow in our ideation skills, our divergent thinking generates more and more rare responses. If a group is surveyed, more than likely the majority of answers would be shared; bowling ball as basketball, bowling ball as workout weight, bowling ball as demolition tool. But with developed creative divergent skills, we begin to see the bowling ball in ways that no one else does. For example, we can imagine the bowling ball as roller skate wheels for an elephant, or a bowling ball as a marble for a giant.

Fourth, increased ideation skills is marked by an increase in the amount of elaboration provided for each idea. For example, we could generate the idea that a bowling ball could act as a replacement head for a doll. A simple idea at its core. But a more creatively advanced idea begins to see outside of the provided box and provide further elaboration. Perhaps the bowling ball head has bowling shoe laces as hair; perhaps the doll has

---

4. The following four categories are drawn from the scoring system of the Torrance Test, a standard test which measures creative ideation abilities.

bowling pins as replacement arms and legs, as well. Increased elaboration often moves outside the provided prompt to imagine a fully elaborated world.

As an individual, we can work to grow our ideation skills in the ways above. And in doing so, we can increase our creative abilities. Yet, if we keep it as only an individual process, we are fundamentally limited. We naturally think within the bounds of our life's experiences and practiced categories. Great creative strides can be made to within this individual box. However, at the end of the day, what we know is what we know; we are limited to the box of our experiences. Therefore, if we are to break free from this box, and foster a fully flourishing creativity, we must look to other boxes by engaging with others.

By opening up our ideation process to others, we quickly become exposed to a whole new set of mental categories and approaches based on a whole different set of life experiences. For one participant who grew up with only brothers, the thought to use a bowling ball as a doll head replacement may never occur to him like his ideation partner who grew up in a household with only sisters. An individual from the American desert would fail to even comprehend that a bowling ball could be used for elephants, while his ideation partner who grew up in the circus in a rainy climate would never even think to drill into the bowling ball and use it as a water storage device. These light-hearted examples demonstrate that collaboration can serve to significantly expand creative horizons.

Creativity scholars have also observed the expanding effect that collaboration has on creativity. Researchers have identified several ways that collaboration expands creativity. Collaboration, in one aspect, is a key source of diversity within the ideation process. Scholars have observed that collaboration benefits the creative process through its ability to bring in a variety of expertise and skill sets to the creative process.[5] Further, creativity researchers have acknowledged that with a higher diversity of opinions, there is a higher likelihood of conflict. But even so, these researchers have identified that dissent within the creative process, while potentially challenging, does in fact lead to a higher level of divergent thinking and creativity.[6] Through collaboration, new creative ideas are formed in higher quantities and with a higher level of quality.[7] Thus overall, these obser-

5. Milliken et al., "Diversity and Creativity," 32–62.

6. Nemeth and Nemeth-Brown, "Better than Individuals," 63–84.

7. Nijstad et al., "Cognitive Stimulation," 137–59.

vations have led some scholars to purport that, despite the legends of individual lone creatives, a creative mind needs the sustained and shared struggles of collaborative thinking in order to generate new ideas and insights.[8] Collaboration is the fuel that sparks an individual's creative fire.

Unfortunately for Liam, it took several strikes of the collaborative flint before a spark caught his creative fire. To his credit, in the class periods that followed Liam's request to be excused from group work, he gave it a good effort. He was engaged, active, and a willing participant. But for a solid two weeks, as he passed my lectern at the end of class, he smiled at me and softly said, "This is not fun." To which I would reply, "Hang in there . . ."

Knowing Liam's angst, I watch his group closely. Their collaborative efforts were playing out all acts of the drama. At times there was silence, which was finally broken by the sharing of an idea. Some member of the group caught the spark and started to riff on the idea. Excitement grew until one or two members poured a cold bucket of dissent on the small fire. Depression would set in, until the cycle returned to silence—effectively starting the cycle over again. But finally, on the third week, a roaring hot blaze came upon the group. The layers of dissent, idea, and counter-idea led them to an idea that was deeply insightful, and so novel in its approach that no single human could have developed it. Expressions of frustration turned into deep smiles and excitement to execute the idea.

As Liam passed my lectern that day, his parting comment changed. He looked me square in the eye and said, "I would have never thought this was possible."

"Exactly, Liam, you could have never thought this possible. It took the unique combination of your group members' experience and skills to come up with this amazing idea. Creativity requires collaboration."

And with a nod of the head, Liam left to work on developing what turned out to be the showcase piece of his portfolio.

UNSELFISH COLLABORATION

The vice of greed is selfish in its tendency to hoard, but perhaps is most selfish in its denial of trust for the provisions provided by God and community. By solely relying on our potential to supply our freedom and security we can achieve some perceived level of success. But like all vices, greed offers

8. John-Steiner, *Creative Collaboration*, 3.

us one thing only to provide us a thin and limited version instead. The security achieved through greed sets a self-imposed perimeter protecting us from the life God may have in store for us. Yet, we snuggle into our hoard, hoping to be free from want, not realizing that we are actually locked into our own golden cage of desires—never really knowing real needs of ourselves and others.

Because greed does provide a thin version of our desires, the act of identifying and pruning it from our character is a difficult task. When greed is present in our lives it does not feel bad; it feels like we need it. Our desires for security and freedom are being fulfilled by it. So when we begin to prune greed, it feels like we are cutting our freedom and our security, leaving only vulnerability.

The process of pruning greed is similar to that of starting a controlled burn within a forest. At first glance, the forest is green and thriving. A casual observer would wonder why the forest ranger plans to burn it down. These questions only become stronger once the ranger sets fire to the forest, leaving only charred remnants of the previously green forest. Looking out over the smoldering ash, we lament at the forest lost. Yet, the forest ranger does not worry, he knows that the forest needed renewal. And sure enough, after a bit of time, the brown turns to green. At first in one spot, then in another. With a short passing of time, the forest flourishes beyond all imagination. Only then do we look back and realize that forest we thought was lush and green was only a fraction of what was possible; and so too it goes with greed. Our sense of security and freedom look lush from greed's offerings. Yet, if we dare to prune, and anticipate with hope the new branches, we are rewarded with a flourishing we could only imagine previously.

With this in mind, it is key to note that the spiritual disciplines for greed may seem counterintuitive and unconstructive. However, it takes trimming greed to reorder our sense of wants and needs—allowing branches of generosity and liberality to emerge. The applied disciplines for greed include the practices of *detachment*[9] and *tithing*.

Detachment

The vice of greed slowly alters our understanding of what is truly necessary, resulting in our sense of attachment to superfluous things. Unfortunately, greed is so persuasive in its ways that we are unable to simply tell ourselves

9. Calhoun, *Spiritual Disciplines Handbook*, 95–98.

that we do not need these things. Thus, the discipline of detachment seeks to discover this truth through physical actions that separate ourselves from the things or ideas we feel like we must have. Ultimately, the goal is to break the grip of greed's false freedom, and begin to experience true freedom; freedom from our disordered desires.

Give Away: One of the most effective ways to begin losing the grip on greed is to practice spontaneous generosity. Thus, this exercise is one of the few exercises that cannot be preplanned. Once ready to practice this discipline, become aware of the desires of the people around you—and be ready and willing to fulfill these desires with your possessions. For example, if while hosting a dinner party one of the guests comments how much they like the table cloth, it is time to practice detachment. After dinner is complete, wipe the table cloth clean, fold it up, and give it to the person. No questions asked. Or in another case, if a classmate comments on how nice your pen set is, cap the pen and hand them the set to keep. Attempt to give with joy, ensuring the recipient that it is okay to accept the gift.

It goes without saying that this exercise will be painful. Most likely you like, and feel like you need, your possessions; you are provided some level of satisfaction by owning them. But with continued practice, the pain will morph into joy as your greed turns to generosity. For success, this exercise requires commitment. It is easy to give away something you don't care about. Start there if necessary, but don't stop until the spontaneous give-away is a sacrifice. Ensure that you are not trying to control the give-away; rather, simply cater to others before yourself.

Creative Reaction: Greed disorders our need for freedom and security in matters of money as well as matters of creativity. In order to practice the discipline of detachment within our creative process, much like above, this exercise seeks to relinquish selfish ownership of your creative practice. In this exercise, invite a trusted individual to provide critique on a creative project. First, present to them your current creative progress, laying out the ideas and development in detail. Ask that they provide feedback on the direction of the final product. Second, describe to them your current creative process. Again, ask them to provide feedback on your process. Inquire what steps they may take next within their process.

After the critique has finished, react to these ideas. Even if it is out of your norm, carry out the next step of the creative process. See where it leads and what value it brings. Additionally, attempt to give full consideration to their critique on the direction of the final outcome. Even if you ultimately reject the idea, give it time and due consideration. Iterate on ideas that tie together the original and suggested idea. Detach from preconceived notions of outcomes or process. Embrace the new stirrings of untidiness. See how creativity expands with collaboration.

Tithing

The discipline of detachment focuses on spontaneous releasing of things you already possess. Similarly the discipline of tithing also seeks to right-size wants versus needs, but accomplishes it in a slightly different manner. Tithing is the act of sacrificing the ability to secure desires in the future through the planned giving of money or creative ownership. This discipline of intentionality prunes greed at its base before it can grow and ensnare through possessions.

Gifts to Church and Charity: Although greed disorders many aspects of our lives, it finds most traction in our attachment to money. This exercise practices the act of seeking freedom and security in the provisions provided by God and community. To begin, over a two-week period of time keep track of all expenditures.[10] After the two weeks, categorize the purchases into two categories "wants" and "needs." Be judicious in your categorization, recognizing that one can live without items that fill a walk-in closet, or fancy takeout meals that constitute a feast in most countries. Tally the amount of money that was spent on "wants." In the following two weeks, try to live on the amount of money used for "needs" in the past two weeks. Next, identify a church or charity which is honorably serving its context. At the end of the second two-week period, take the money that you would have normally spent on wants, but saved, and donate it to the church or charity.

After this initial intense exercise in the rightsizing of monetary wants, carry out a second part of the exercise the following month. In this second part, identify an amount of money that you would be willing to donate to the church or charity each month, for a period of three months. The actual amount is not of detailed concern. Rather, whatever amount is chosen should be a sacrifice. Or in other words, it should hurt a bit to give that specific amount of money away. If it does not affect you, increase the amount until it does. Over the next three months, donate that exact sum at

10. DeYoung, *Glittering Vices*, 113–16.

the first of each month. At the end of three months, reflect on any change in attitude toward giving. Evaluate whether you really missed the money once you were in a pattern of giving. Rather, let yourself feel the joy of generosity.

Idea Offering: Money represents our ability to secure our own sense of freedom and security. But within the creative process, ownership of ideas and process represents our ability to control and express our voice. To counter this limited notion of creativity, seek to intentionally tithe your ideas for the betterment of others. In this exercise, identify a group creative project, or a creative project where others are simultaneously participating and producing alternative proposals. Predetermine to share the best ideas and craft secrets with others.

As the project begins, invite other creative individuals working on the project to discuss initial ideas. Be generous in speaking about what you feel are your best ideas. Openly preface your offering with statements like, "I don't own this idea, so anyone is welcome to take it and run with it if they feel it has legs." Such statements ensure that a greedy heart condition stays in check, even if no one works on the idea further. During the process, mentally picture giving the idea away—releasing control of it. Reflect on any feelings of insecurity or loss of freedom. Question whether your generosity of ideas really damaged your ability to carry out a flourishing creative process.

In all the disciplines above, the aim is to intentionally put desire of virtue over immediate fulfillment through hoarding. Losing the grip of greed will fail without such intentionality. Yet, if we are successful we may lean on, for the first time, trust in the provision of God and community. And with this trust, we in turn receive a more flourishing creative life than we could ever imagine.

• • •

Greed is a trap. It lures with promises of fulfillment via control and acquisitions; yet leaves only a limited kingdom that rules its owner. We think that our lives and our creativity are at their fullest when we shape them through self-focused efforts to obtain security and freedom. But in reality this false perception is the definition of the invisible shackles of greed's reign.

Fortunately for Liam, through creative collaboration, he was able to get a small glimpse of what life could be like free from greed's grasp. He realized that his perception of creative success was limited, soothed into complacency by the comfort of control. Only when he accepted the untidiness that comes with creative collaboration did he see new horizons of creative flourishing.

8

The Humble Creative

WHO WE ARE AFFECTS our creativity. Our moral character can either lead to disordered creativity or cultivate a creativity that flourishes.

The stories throughout this book tell this tale; warning us that a life defined by vice creates deep challenges for the creative process. Whether derived from adherence to an ethic of authenticity, or simply emerging from our fallen natures, a life of vice sacrifices successful creativity on the altar of selfish desires. Vainglory, envy, sloth, anger, lust of the eyes, and greed poison our character and choke our creativity.

Yet despite the destructive nature of these specific vices, there is an even more fundamentally destructive vice that undergirds all other vices. The monastic use of a tree to describe a vice-laden life illustrates this well. A vice tree has multiple parts that attribute to its demise. The poisoned fruit is the most obviously sickened part of the tree. But the fruit grows from the visible vice-laden twisted branches. However, the real source of the tree's sickness is not visible to the eye at all. The bad fruit and twisted branches are not the entirety of the tree. The source of the tree's life comes from its roots, which firmly anchor it and provide its life source. In the case of a vice-laden tree, the roots—the very parts that cause the tree to develop its character—are pride.

Each chapter, each vice, and each story of creative struggle comes back to prideful roots. When we place ourselves at the center and source of existence, denying any external source of good and right, we grow prideful roots. When we magnify our natural love for ourselves to a level such that our actions become unspoken sentiments of disdain or indifference of others, we grow prideful roots. When we think more highly of ourselves than is just, we grow prideful roots. When we perceive our natural desires as the source of all things right, we grow prideful roots. When we seek to diagnose the source of our creative disorder, understanding the role of specific vices is important—but recognizing pride is essential.

If we are willing and able to recognize our pride, we take the first step to changing our roots. The mere act of identifying pride is a simultaneous act of establishing virtuous roots—roots of humility. Just as prideful roots infect the entirety of the tree, roots of humility begin to grow a tree defined by straight branches of virtue that produce life-giving fruit. And in our specific case, roots of humility are foundational to the cultivation of flourishing creativity.

The majority of this book has been dedicated to illuminating the telltale sources, symptoms, and effects of vice on creativity. By understanding vice and how it manifests, we are able to successfully start pruning as an act of spiritual and moral formation. But if we do not intentionally attend to the roots, no matter how many vice branches we trim, they will grow back with time. Therefore, in order to make positive headway to cultivating flourishing creativity, we must also begin to develop humility in our lives.

What follows is a code, of sorts, which delineates a description of a creative life defined by humility. Formulated into a list of propositions, this creative humility code attempts to simplify what is, in reality, the manifestation of a very long journey that requires active partnership with God and the receiving of abundant grace. Despite its limitations, the code provides a coherent picture of the humble roots necessary for a life of flourishing creativity.

THE HUMBLE CREATIVE

The life of a humble creative is defined by the:

1. Recognition that goodness, truth, and beauty exist—and that no single human is the fullest manifestation of these transcendentals. Our natures are fundamentally fallen in practice, and thus in essence fall short of perfection. Therefore, our instinctual desires do not define goodness, truth, or beauty.

2. Acceptance that the ultimate source of right and good cannot be defined by a fallen human nature. Instead we must look to external sources. Such sources include proven wisdom stemming from family, ancestors, rules, traditions, institutions, exemplars, and fundamentally God himself.

3. Understanding that fallen instinctual desires must be shaped by these external sources of right and good. Refinement does not happen on its own, but takes intentional recognition, development, and partnership with God. No matter how much effort is put into refining a fallen nature, the sick cannot heal the sick. Any true moral development is spiritual development stemming from God's grace.

4. Assurance that, despite a fallen nature, humanity is made in the *imago Dei*—or image of God—thus acknowledging that life has the innate ability to mirror God's attributes. Such attributes include love, goodness, mercy, righteousness, truthfulness, self-control—and creativity.

5. Realization that life's main goal is not to selfishly please our innate desires. A life best lived is a life that fully participates in the drama of becoming more virtuous and Christlike. And thus success in life is defined by who we are and how well we love—not by our achievements, accumulation of possessions, or fulfillment of hedonistic pleasure.

6. Commitment to avoid making oneself the center of the universe by seeking a life defined by loving God and loving one's neighbors. Such a life is characterized by joyful service, purposeful sacrifice, and the intentional sharing of goodness, truth, and beauty.

7. Desire to align one's creative purpose, and creative process, to the broader life commitments above.

8. Willingness to secure one's identity in God's assurances and not the popular acceptance of creative works, or conflating creative works with personal identity—thus, exemplifying a creative process that is free to explore, experiment, and ultimately fail.

9. Dedication to carrying out a creative process that fulfills the demands of love. Such a process places the other before one's creative ideas—defining creativity through empathetic care and love.

10. Ability to seek goodness, truth, and beauty over and above the temptation to explore the illicit within the creative process. Such creativity

does not seek novelty for novelty's sake, but aims to really understand creation and the Creator well.

11. Appreciation of other creative individuals' talents and successes— avoiding the corresponding feelings of doubt, insecurity, and bitterness; celebrating the success of other creative works for their role in bringing goodness, truth, and beauty into view.

12. Proclivity to share ideas and collaborate within the creative process— knowing that the ultimate end of creativity is not self-glory, but a reconciliation of creation. Such a creativity prioritizes the duty to act as an agent of reconciliation in this world, over and above the security of ownership.

13. Acknowledgment that reaching such a level of flourishing creativity is not a one-and-done event. Rather, it is a long faithfulness in the same direction of pursuing humility, virtue, and Christlikeness.[1] Such a faithfulness knows that a life without intentionally, and God's grace, will naturally drift toward vice.

14. Appreciation that living out a life defined by this humility code is fundamentally countercultural. Yet, despite the narrow path, the hope and longing for a flourishing creativity catalyzes action toward becoming a humble creative.

• • •

The message of this book is that the contemporary creative culture fosters vice within individuals, causing their creativity to become disordered. Throughout the book we have explored the specific vice-laden temptations that we all face. And with the aid of the long-standing Christian tradition of moral formation, we have recognized that the first step toward virtue and Christlikeness is recognition of vice in our lives. So perhaps for the first time we recognize our vices: we see the pride that forms our roots; we notice the twisted branches poisoning our fruit; we glimpse the potentiality and potency of virtue; and we start to lament the thinness of a vice-laden creativity. And with this recognition, the Christian tradition of moral and spiritual formation has begun.

1. This statement is a riff on Eugene Peterson's notion of "a long obedience in the same direction" (Peterson, *Long Obedience*).

But we do not stop at simple recognition. Acknowledging vice in our lives prompts us forward, now with a clearer vision of the path that leads to Christlike character and a life well lived. Yet, as this Christian tradition frequently implores, the next steps forward are "not a self-help project but a Spirit-empowered movement."[2] We must humbly admit, and submit, our pride to God, seeking his grace and empowerment to pursue virtue. And while doing so, we must recognize that a reliance on God's grace is license for us to sit back and be passive in the process. Pruning vice from our tree of life takes an intentional, energetic, focused effort—alongside God's formative action.[3]

So with the longing and hope of a flourishing life, and flourishing creativity, we humbly reorder our desires and loves—praying regularly as St. Augustine did, "Order me in my love," oh God, "Order me in my love."[4]

2. DeYoung, *Glittering Vices*, 182.

3. DeYoung, *Glittering Vices*, 182.

4. Augustine, *City of God*, XV.22, 29.

Bibliography

Adkins, Chris. "How Does Empathy Influence Creativity." https://dlibrary.stanford.edu/questions/how-does-empathy-influence-creativity.

Augustine. *The City of God.* Translated by Demetrius B. Zema et al. Washington, DC: Catholic University of America Press, 2008.

———. *Confessions of St. Augustine.* Auckland: Floating, 1921.

Aquinas, Thomas. *On Evil.* Edited by Brian Davies. Oxford: Oxford University Press, 2003.

———. *Summa Theologica.* Translated by Fathers of the English Dominican Province. Westminster: Christian Classics, 1981.

Atkinson, John. *An Introduction to Motivation.* New York: American Book, 1964.

Baehr, Jason. "Open-Mindedness." In *Being Good: Christian Virtues for Everyday Life,* edited by Michael W. Austin and R. Douglas Geivett, 30–52. Grand Rapids: Eerdmans, 2012.

———. "The Structure of Open-Mindedness." *Canadian Journal of Philosophy* 41 (2011) 191–213.

Bass, Matthijs, et al. "A Meta-Analysis of 25 Years of Mood-Creativity Research: Hedonic Tone Activation, or Regulatory Focus?" *Psychological Bulletin* 134 (2008) 779–806.

Baumgarten, Elias. "Curiosity as a Moral Virtue." *International Journal of Applied Philosophy* 15 (2001) 169–84.

Bell, Chloe E., and Steven J. Robbins. "Effect of Art Production on Negative Mood: A Randomized, Controlled Trial." *Art Therapy* 24 (2007) 71–75.

Bellah, Robert, et al. *Habits of the Heart: Individualism and Commitment in American Life.* Berkley: University of California Press, 1985.

Calhoun, Adele. *Spiritual Disciplines Handbook: Practices That Transform Us.* Downers Grove: InterVarsity, 2005.

Cassian, John. *Institutes.* Translated by Boniface Ramsey. New York: Newman, 2000.

Csikszentmihalyi, Mihaly. *Creativity: Flow and the Psychology of Discovery and Invention.* New York: HarperCollins, 1996.

Cook, Jeff. *Seven: The Deadly Sins and the Beatitudes.* Grand Rapids: Zondervan, 2008.

Conner, Tamlin S., et al. "Everyday Creative Activity as a Path to Flourishing." *Journal of Positive Psychology* 13 (2018) 181–89.

Cropley, Arthur. "Fostering Creativity in the Classroom: General Principles." In *The Creativity Research Handbook,* vol. 1, edited by Mark A. Runco, 83–114. Cresskill, NJ: Hampton, 1997.

Dacey, John, et al. *Understanding Creativity: The Interplay of Biological, Psychological, and Social Factors.* San Francisco: Jossey-Bass, 1998.

DeYoung, Colin G. "Openness/Intellect: A Dimension of Personality Reflecting Cognitive Exploration." In *A Handbook of Personality and Social Psychology: Personality Processes and Individual Differences*, vol. 4, edited by M. L. Cooper and R. J. Larsen, 369–99. Washington, DC: American Psychological Association, 2014.

DeYoung, Rebecca Konyndyk. *Glittering Vices: A New Look at the Seven Deadly Sins and Their Remedies*. Grand Rapids: Brazos, 2009.

Forgeard, Marie J. C., and Katherine V. Eichner. "Creativity as a Target and Tool for Positive Interventions." In *The Wiley Blackwell Handbook of Positive Psychological Interventions*, edited by Acacia C. Parks and Stephen M. Schueller, 137–54. Oxford: Wiley Blackwell, 2014.

Form, Sven, and Christian Kaernbach. "More Is Not Always Better: The Differentiated Influence of Empathy on Different Magnitudes of Creativity." *Europe's Journal of Psychology* 14 (2018) 54–65.

Foster, Richard. *The Freedom of Simplicity*. New York: HarperCollins, 1981.

Gardner, Howard. "Creativity: An Interdisciplinary Perspective." *Creativity Research Journal* 1 (1988) 8–26.

Getzels, Jacob W. "Creativity: Process and Issues." In *Perspectives in Creativity*, edited by Irving A. Taylor and Jacob W. Getzels, 326–44. Hawthorne, NY: Aldine, 1975.

Grant, Adam M., et al. "The Necessity of Others Is the Mother of Invention: Intrinsic and Prosocial Motivations, Perspective Taking, and Creativity." *Academy of Management Journal* 54 (2011) 73–96.

Guinness, Os. *The Call: Finding and Fulfilling God's Purpose for Your Life*. Nashville: Nelson, 2018.

Hardy, Jay H., et al. "Outside the Box: Epistemic Curiosity as a Predictor of Creative Problem Solving and Creative Performance." *Personality and Individual Differences* 104 (2017) 230–37.

Jay, E., and David Perkins. "Problem Finding: The Search for Mechanism." In *The Creativity Research Handbook*, vol. 1, edited by Mark A. Runco, 257–93. Cresskill, NJ: Hampton, 1997.

John-Steiner, Vera. *Creative Collaboration*. New York: Oxford University Press, 2000.

Kaufman, Scott Barry, et al. "Openness to Experience and Intellect Differentially Predict Creative Achievement in the Arts and Sciences." *Journal of Personality* 84 (2016) 248–58.

Keller, Tim. *Preaching: Communicating Faith in an Age of Skepticism*. New York: Penguin, 2016.

Kelley, Tom, and David Kelley. *Creative Confidence: Unleashing the Creative Potential within Us All*. London: William Collins, 2015.

MacKinnon, Donald W. *In Search of Human Effectiveness: Identifying and Developing Creativity*. Buffalo: Creative Education Foundation, 1978.

May, Rollo. *The Courage to Create*. Toronto: Peter Smith, 1985.

Mayer, Richard E. "Fifty Years of Creativity Research." In *Handbook of Creativity*, edited by Robert J. Stenberg, 449–60. New York: Cambridge University Press, 1999.

Meilaender, Gilbert. *The Theory and Practice of Virtue*. Notre Dame: University of Notre Dame Press, 2006.

Milliken, Frances, et al. "Diversity and Creativity in Work Groups: A Dynamic Perspective of the Affective and Cognitive Processes That Link Diversity and Performance." In *Group Creativity: Innovation through Collaboration*, edited by Bernard Arjan Nijstad and Paul B Paulus, 32–62. New York: Oxford University Press, 2003.

Nemeth, Charlan, and Brendan Nemeth-Brown. "Better than Individuals? The Potential Benefits of Dissent and Diversity for Group Creativity." In *Group Creativity: Innovation through Collaboration*, edited by Bernard Arjan Nijstad and Paul B. Paulus, 63–84. New York: Oxford University Press, 2003.

Nijstad, Bernard Arjan, et al. "Cognitive Stimulation and Interface in Idea-Generating Groups." In *Group Creativity: Innovation through Collaboration*, edited by Bernard Arjan Nijstad and Paul B. Paulus, 137–59. New York: Oxford University Press, 2003.

Perkins, D. N. *The Mind's Best Work*. Cambridge: Harvard University Press, 1981.

Peterson, Eugene. *A Long Obedience in the Same Direction: Discipleship in an Instant Society*. Downers Grove: InterVarsity, 1980.

Peterson, Jordan B., et al. "Openness and Extraversion Are Associated with Reduced Latent Inhibition: Replication and Commentary." *Personality and Individual Differences* 33 (2002) 1137–47.

Petrone, Paul. "Why Creativity Is the Most Important Skill in the World." LinkedIn Learning Blog, December 31, 2018. https://learning.linkedin.com/blog/top-skills/why-creativity-is-the-most-important-skill-in-the-world.

Rasulzada, Farida, and Ingrid Dackert. "Organizational Creativity and Innovation in Relation to Psychological Well-Being and Organizational Factors." *Creativity Research Journal* 21 (2009) 191–98.

Rokeach, Milton. "In Pursuit of the Creative Process." In *The Creative Organization*, edited by Gary Albert Steiner, 66–88. Chicago: University of Chicago Press, 1965.

Ryan, Richard M., and Edward L. Deci. "On Happiness and Human Potentials: A Review of Research on Hedonic and Eudiamonic Well-Being." *Annual Review of Psychology* 52 (2001) 141–66.

Sarnoff, David P., and Henry P. Cole. "Creative and Personal Growth." *Journal of Creative Behavior* 17 (1983) 95–102.

Shekerjian, Denise. *Uncommon Genius: How Great Ideas Are Born*. New York: Penguin, 1991.

Silvia, Paul J., et al. "Assessing Creativity with Divergent Thinking Tasks: Exploring the Reliability and Validity of New Subjective Scoring Methods." *Psychology of Aesthetics, Creativity, and the Arts* 2 (2008) 68–85.

Sternberg, Robert J., and Todd I. Lubart. *Defying the Crowd: Cultivating Creativity in a Culture of Conformity*. New York: Free Press, 1995.

Sternberg, Robert J., et al. *The Creativity Conundrum: A Propulsion Model of Kinds of Creative Contributions*. New York: Psychology, 2002.

Taylor, Charles. *The Ethics of Authenticity*. Cambridge: Harvard University Press, 1991.

———. *Sources of the Self: The Making of the Modern Identity*. Cambridge: Harvard University Press, 2012.

Tharp, Twyla. *The Creative Habit: Learn It and Use It for Life*. New York: Simon & Schuster, 2006.

Torrance, E. Paul. *The Search for Satori and Creativity*. Buffalo: Creative Education Foundation, 1979.

———. *Why Fly? A Philosophy of Creativity*. Norwood, NJ: Ablex, 1995.

Williams, David. "10 Things Highly Authentic Creatives Do Differently." *Web Writer Spotlight*, July 26, 2018. https://webwriterspotlight.com/10-things-highly-authentic-creatives-do-differently.

Winner, Ellen. *Gifted Children: Myths and Realities*. New York: Basic, 1996.

Wright, T. A., and Andre P. Walton. "Affect, Psychological Well-Being and Creativity: Results of a Field Study." *Journal of Business and Management* 9 (2003) 21–32.

Zhu, Pearl. "Creativity and Authenticity." *Future of CIO* (blog). https://futureofcio. blogspot.com/2019/01/creativity-and-authenticity.html.